Praise for *Ministry to the Incarcerated*

"In my seventeen years of prison ministry, I have never seen a book so sensitively written about prisons and prisoners. I rode on a roller coaster of emotions as Dr. Covert's writing demanded that I not just look at the situation, but actually become a part of it while reading. This book needs to be read by everyone who is involved or thinking about getting involved in prison ministry."

—**REV. NICK BARBETTA,** *Executive Director, Crossroads Prison Ministries*

"A timely message juxtaposed to the political rhetoric and public mood of today. . . . Reverend Covert's treatment of the challenges of ministry in prisons is insightful in describing both the uniqueness of the environment and the role of the church in it. His book should be read by chaplains, prison staff, inmates, and policymakers— especially those who seek to make these environments "harsher" and "meaner.""

—**JOSEPH D. LEHMAN,** *Commissioner, Maine Department of Corrections*

"*Ministry to the Incarcerated* gives excellent materials for understanding the correctional system in which both chaplains and volunteers are ministering. . . . Specific teaching and training dealing with the "Inmate Stressors" is an example of subjects that help prepare prisoners for their return to society. I would recommend [Dr. Covert's] book be used in the training of new chaplains and in the orientation of volunteers coming into jail and prison ministry. His insights will help prevent some of the common errors of judgment made by newcomers to the correctional setting."

—**RICK DAVIS,** *minister in military, correctional, hospital, and industrial settings, Industrial and Institutional Chaplaincy, The General Council of the Assemblies of God*

"Valuable supplemental reading for students considering employment within the criminal justice system, Covert's *Ministry to the Incarcerated* focuses on the basic human needs of inmates, delineates the roadblocks that hinder prisoners' personal and spiritual growth and development, and offers concrete suggestions that would tear down the roadblocks and promote positive change. . . . The detailed curriculum outlines found in the appendix would be especially helpful to those considering prison ministry; however, anyone who works within the prison system would benefit from reading Covert's book and seeing the prison system from the eyes of those who live there."

—**DIANA L. KUHNS,** *Director of the Integrated Studies Division, Pennsylvania College of Technology, Penn State*

"*Ministry to the Incarcerated* is a clear, comprehensive introduction to effective ministry within the prison system. Obviously based on years of experience, it presents the problems and pressures of prison in a way that would keep a new chaplain from many mistakes and make his counseling much more realistic. Beyond that, it gives fresh and thoughtful suggestions for bringing the Christian faith alive for one of the more neglected groups of our population. It is an eye-opener, a heart opener, and an encouragement."

—**REV. JAMES PETERSON,** *Office of the Marginalized, Diocese of Erie Catholic Charities*

Ministry to the Incarcerated

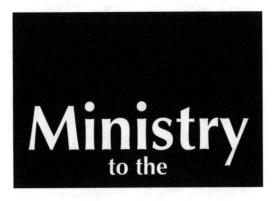

Ministry
to the

Incarcerated

Henry G. Covert

Loyola
Press
Chicago

Loyola Press
3441 North Ashland Avenue
Chicago, Illinois 60657

Cover design by Frederick Falkenberg.
Cover art by Bob Masheris.
Cover photograph from Tony Stone Images.
Interior design by Tammi Longsjo.

Excerpts from BASIC TYPES OF PASTORAL CARE & COUNSELING: RESOURCES FOR THE MINISTRY OF HEALING AND GROWTH, Howard Clinebell. Copyright ©1966 and 1984 by Abingdon Press. Used with permission.

Excerpts from THE CHURCH IN THE POWER OF THE SPIRIT by JURGEN MOLTMANN. English translation copyright (c) 1977 by SCM Press, Ltd. Reprinted by permission of HarperCollins Publishers, Inc.

Excerpts from THE CRUCIFIED GOD by JURGEN MOTLMANN. English translation copyright (c) 1974 by SCM Press Ltd. Reprinted by permission of HarperCollins Publishers, Inc.

Excerpts from THE SEARCH FOR COMPASSION: Spirituality and Ministry by Andrew Purves. ©1989 Andrew Purves. Used by permission of Westminister/John Knox Press.

Library of Congress Cataloging-in-Publication Data

Covert, Henry G.
    Ministry to the incarcerated / Henry G. Covert
    p.   cm.
    Includes bibliographical references and index.
    ISBN 0-8294-0860-6 (alk. paper)
    1. Church work with prisoners.   2. Prisoners—Religious life.
I. Title.
BV4340.C68 1995
259'.5—dc20   95-8780
                                                              CIP

Contents

92571

Preface

Prison chaplains work with offenders and staff on many levels. Their extensive responsibilities and mobility within the prison bring them into contact with every conceivable situation, which enables them to discover and examine the latent forces that exist in the prison setting. In other words, chaplains are privy to the beliefs, feelings, and emotions that lie below the surface.

This book is intended to provide an understanding of the incarcerated and their environment. It proposes to create insights, for both criminal justice professionals and the general public, that will stimulate reflection on the present condition of the correctional system and imprisoned felons. Awareness is the beginning of positive change.

Ministry to the Incarcerated addresses individuals who have "crossed over" the moral and legal bounds of society and the system that is charged with their custody and care. The following chapters do not take sides; rather, they set forth the personal and environmental realities of prison life and show how they impact inmate development. Chapter 1 is an introduction to these dynamics.

The central difficulty for inmates is personal growth. When we consider the many tensions in a prisoner's life, we begin to understand this. Regardless of how we define human development, the penal environment unquestionably presents unyielding obstacles. While incarceration certainly encourages personal change, prison remains a difficult place to experience divine grace and significant maturation. We will examine some of these obstacles to personal growth in chapter 2.

Chapter 3 looks at three paradigms for prison ministry: the dimensions of the cross, the ministry of presence, and the priesthood of servants. These models provide meaning and spiritual identification for individuals who are serving prison sentences. Their content, various dimensions, and flexibility help break through the stress-related obstacles of incarceration, thus stimulating emotional and spiritual formation. The appendix contains curriculum outlines to help combat the obstacles to prison ministry.

Finally, chapter 4 examines secular needs that are directly related to stress and negative attitudes; therefore, they must be confronted seriously by prison administrators. Most of these needs are associated with living conditions and programs. Correcting these problems would improve inmate outlook and behavior.

This book integrates what I have learned through my careers as a police officer and a prison chaplain and what my own research has revealed. The information it contains is a result of extensive interaction with prisoners in both private and group settings, and reflects over five thousand conversations with inmates, prison volunteers, and other chaplains.

Rev. Dr. Henry G. Covert, Chaplain
State Correctional Institution at Rockview
Bellefonte, Pennsylvania

Acknowledgments

This book is dedicated to the incarcerated, many of whom desperately seek forgiveness and the rehabilitative tools necessary for a new life. The following research represents their voices and needs. I am especially grateful to the inmates at the State Correctional Institution at Rockview for their insights and honest expressions.

Special thanks to Dr. Joseph F. Mazurkiewicz, the superintendent at SCI Rockview, and Deputy John McCullough. These men are truly concerned about the welfare of prison inmates, and their expertise and empathy have resulted in numerous improvements at the Rockview facility. Deep appreciation is also extended to my wife, Katherine, whose continuous encouragement and support enabled me to complete this project.

My hope is that the insights given in this book will redirect our thinking about the incarcerated—a segment of society that is often misunderstood and forgotten. May God add his blessings to these efforts and all glory be given to Christ our Lord, who wills that none perish and that all come to repentance and eternal life.

Introduction

Penal institutions communicate few positive messages to society. In fact, in most community and political circles they are unpopular subjects for discussion. The problems in county, state, and federal prisons are an increasing concern for everyone. Prisons obliterate the landscape, intimidate communities, and create a financial burden for governments. These forbidding structures are also a constant reminder of the increasing crime rate and of our inability to solve this troublesome problem.

Today, issues of crime and punishment are paramount, and it is difficult to envision rapid changes in a prison system that has historically been one of warehousing and punishment. Institutional improvement inevitably requires changes in personal, societal, and political attitudes and philosophies. When we consider the magnitude of these factors it is easy to join those who simply close their eyes to an unpleasant and seemingly impossible situation. Such apathy, however, develops like an infectious and terminal cancer.

Many people think that society's ills are impossible to cure, but humanitarian efforts can have positive results, even with problems of crime and imprisonment. Although crime is a deeply-rooted and complex problem, positive steps can be taken to improve the situation. There is no room for those with defeatist attitudes—this response is superficial. The incarcerated must be understood in terms of healing and rehabilitation, and this requires a collective effort from society to promote compassion, self-worth, and hope.

Regardless how we interpret the Genesis account of sin, the corrupt nature of humanity cannot be disputed. Yet, liberation theology reveals a God who frees humanity from the power of sin through transforming love. This liberation is not an abstract thought but, rather, a divine and personal force in the human experience. The birth of restoring grace is offered to the worst of sinners. Convicted felons can change, and this message must be communicated to society.

God became involved in the human struggle through the Incarnation. Jesus willfully entered life's "prisons," penetrating the alleys of bitterness and despair with the desire and power to set captives free. He came as a servant, preaching the good news of forgiveness, reconciliation, and healing through the love of a merciful creator. Jesus' message promised liberation from the sinful self for both the oppressed and the oppressor. He was concerned with the whole person, and those touched by him attested to his miraculous healing.

The church must follow the exemplary life of Christ. But this presents a crucial question: What does it mean to follow Jesus Christ? Dietrich Bonhoeffer said, "When Christ calls someone, he bids that person come and Christ's grace is not cheap, but demanding" (Dulles 1974, 225). In other words, taking up the cross means a death to self-serving will and an acceptance of the responsibility and pain that accompanies identification and involvement with the oppressed. We must move beyond rhetoric and concern to concrete forms of action. We are called to touch the lives of others through the grace given to us. Such grace may even come through the sensitivity and understanding created by our own imperfections and wounds.

God's forgiving and transforming grace is everywhere, regardless of the intensity of sin and perceived hopelessness. This grace has no bounds, and it has the power to penetrate any depth. One cannot believe in God's healing grace and at the same time cast aside the incarcerated.

1

Ministry in an
Adverse Environment

The Dynamics of Prison Ministry

Rather than give a detailed description of prison ministry in this chapter, it seems more appropriate to provide some of my personal insights and concerns. As we progress through the book you will come to see the larger picture of prison chaplaincy, especially the diverse responsibilities of chaplains and the obstacles to their ministry.

Explaining prison ministry is difficult because of its uniqueness. Every prison chaplain encounters different ethical questions. For example, clergy working in facilities that have a death row are confronted with questions about capital punishment and equal justice. Because the State Correctional Institution at Rockview is the designated location for executions in Pennsylvania, I have been forced to work through my own convictions on this subject. But every chaplain must deal with the daily struggles of human need in the midst of a dehumanizing and punishing environment.

Prison ministry is unquestionably a challenging and stressful profession. My years in law enforcement cannot be compared to the daily stress of working in a large correctional facility. Prison clergy are faced with every conceivable problem, all of which demand some manner of response. In the adverse environment of prision the extremes of life are acted out in unpredictable ways. Inmate mistrust and anger produce an emotional instability that is simply impossible to measure or anticipate.

Ministry to convicted felons necessitates being attentive to individual and group dynamics, including the moods of particular groups as they relate to the total community. This sensitivity is not only important to pastoral care, but it also addresses security and safety concerns. An awareness of the latent forces that exist in prisons can lead to administrative decisions that will prevent confrontations.

Working with inmates has led me to examine my own emotions. The demands placed on chaplains are a test of character and spirituality, and through honest self-examination I have learned some displeasing truths about myself—intolerance of certain personality types stands in the foreground. Institutional pastors spend considerable time with many objectionable people, and it is easy to build walls against particular types of individuals. It is imperative, therefore, that prison chaplains continuously examine their motives.

Stress associated with imprisonment produces relentless frustration and rage in inmates, and some of this is projected onto pastors. I have never been threatened by a prisoner, but I have frequently been the recipient of explosive anger. Crisis intervention is a daily part of prison ministry, and it demands enormous energy and discipline.

Whatever the circumstances, chaplains must use caution when communicating with the incarcerated. Many prisoners have a poor self-image that makes them defensive. As such, they are very conscious of the language, tone of voice, and attitudes of others. My experience reveals that felons can usually accept disappointments if staff members express concern. Giving a brief explanation, offering alternatives, and integrating something positive can go a long way in eliminating inmate tensions and improving relationships between inmates and staff.

The most common problem in prison is the incessant environmental stress, which is heightened when inmates are experiencing additional personal problems. Forcing troubled and angry people to live in the isolated confinement of a highly-structured system can lead to jealousy, self-elevation, and anger.

The incarcerated live in a very small world; hence, they are very aware of their surroundings. They spend countless hours observing their peers and prison staff with a critical eye. Many offenders are judgmental of their fellow residents. Criticism of others seems to help them cope with their own guilt and pain. Some prisoners work hard to elevate themselves at the expense of others, and chaplains are often sounding boards for inmates making harsh judgments about their peers.

Unlike neighborhood pastors, prison chaplains are in the midst of their parishioners every day. Also, their work is not confined to one faith group but, rather, the entire inmate community. Rockview has more than two thousand prisoners and only two full-time chaplains. However, with scheduled days off there is only one chaplain on duty four days of the week. Contract clergy and volunteers are available for some religious groups, but they only enter the institution for worship services and studies. This is the structure of religious programming in most prisons, and it places a heavy burden on chaplains.

As one would expect, there is little time for follow-up work with offenders, which is a dilemma for the many dependent personalities who see clergy as their main source of attention, encouragement, and support. Pastors have a limited amount of time to spend with inmates, and this lack of attention upsets individuals whose concept of pastoral care includes monopolizing the chaplain's time.

Being a chaplain to an entire prison community embraces all the distortions and extremes affiliated with these individuals and groups. Prisons could not possibly employ full-time chaplains for each faith group; therefore, those who are employed must serve as coordinators for all religions. They must organize functions and make spiritual decisions for each individual religion, which requires a working knowledge of all practicing faiths.

Added to this melting-pot ministry are institutional rules and restrictions relating to security and safety. Chaplains are constantly reminded by administrators that they are pastors of a prison congregation, meaning that security always takes precedence. While such conditions are understood by clergy, they often hamper certain forms of ministry. Pastors characteristically try to meet the needs of their parishioners, but institutional rules frequently make it impossible to do so. Needless to say, it can be very frustrating.

The inability to meet many inmate needs causes stress for those in ministry. Natural responses for pastors in other settings are often prohibited in prison. The uniqueness of the penal environment dictates the methodology and limitations of ministry. Pastors cannot engage in any activity that may cause institutional or legal difficulties, and they must be careful to function within the scope of their department. A minister's adherence to administrative mandates requires acceptance of the rules, discipline, and an understanding that security and safety are the top priorities in prison. To prevent violating institutional rules chaplains must continuously reexamine existing policies. The interpretation of these policies means networking with security and treatment personnel.

Most of the requests that prison clergy receive from inmates are not of a spiritual nature. The church is viewed by many offenders as an avenue of last resort, which opens the door to virtually every type of problem. When inmate frustration levels reach a crisis point, the chaplain usually becomes an object of ventilation. However, chaplains are often unable to change an inmate's situation, which sometimes causes prisoners to develop negative attitudes toward the church.

Some residents view the church as nothing more than a branch of the legal system. Inmates are often suspicious of prison ministry, believing that chaplains are just part of an apathetic and oppressive system. These individuals join the ranks of other felons who contend that the church can do nothing for them. Although similar attitudes are found in other ministries, they are distinct in prison. Chaplains must accept that such attitudes will always exist in the penal setting.

Church authority is another stumbling block for some offenders. A significant number of convicted criminals detest authority of any kind, and this attitude carries over to the church. Authority problems resist easy solutions. In the majority of cases prisoners react to authority with unconscious responses that have been nurtured over the years. As such, the church can only build trust through a progressive and consistently compassionate presence.

Crime-related confessions present other concerns for institutional clergy. Offenders sometimes come to chaplains with disclosures of their past crimes, or even crimes that they have committed during their incarceration. Residents also offer information pertaining to the illegal activities of others. Such knowledge obviously places institutional pastors in an awkward position. While institutional rules and state laws are clear concerning knowledge of criminal activity, they contradict the conscience of some clergy. Prison rules dictate that chaplains report all illegal activity, but adhering to such rules can affect the credibility of both the chaplain and the church. When the church assumes the additional role of correctional officer, something is lost in terms of essence and purpose. In the prison setting the church is caught between the tensions of mercy and law.

While the church and the state have similar mission statements, they differ in their interpretation of events, understanding of priorities, and perception of rehabilitation. The spiritual aspect of the church places it in a category apart from all correctional departments, which can in itself create areas of friction with staff members.

However, the church normally receives cooperation from prison staff. Most supervisors recognize that ministry has a positive role to play in penal communities. Nonetheless, some staff members view prison chaplains as being naive, unrealistic victims of inmate power and manipulation. Although few in number, these employees believe that inmates have no right to worship or be assisted by the church.

Tensions become more complex when staff members bring their personal problems into the institution. Troubled employees sometimes translate their frustrations into prisoner abuse, and chaplains find themselves in the middle. Most correctional employees resist harassing inmates, but every prison has some vexatious staff members who cause relational turmoil. Many of these problems could be prevented or kept to a minimum by implementing training seminars for staff that focus on pertinent topics, such as cultural diversity and conflict resolution. Yet, staff education is not a priority in the prison system, and this lack of wisdom continues to take its toll.

Although many institutions claim to promote rehabilitation, they remain demeaning environments. Prisoners find themselves in a system that does little to provide the incentives and resources that facilitate personal change. But the problem goes much deeper than apathetic and insufficiently trained staff members—it is rooted in a society whose prison philosophy is revenge and punishment.

Determining Successful Ministry

Correctional chaplains must redefine successful ministry. Denominations and local churches use various statistics, such as attendance, to measure success, but these methods are insufficient in penal institutions where everything is in flux. Emotional instability, strong peer influences, spiritual misconceptions and distortions, and changing populations all influence statistical fluctuation.

But regardless of the type of ministry, statistics provide little evidence of spiritual development. Attendance records and other statistics may indicate community needs, but they do not measure personal growth. Some inmates attend counseling sessions, worship services, and Bible studies for other than spiritual reasons—they may expect something in return for attendance.

Having served both local parishes and prison communities, I am convinced that success in ministry can only be understood in the context of *pastoral spirituality*. Success does not center around programs, budgets, and statistics, but around intent, willingness, and commitment. Personal charisma and large ministries are not as important as a compassionate presence made possible through the indwelling Spirit. Simply stated, successful ministry is found in the willingness to experience pain for the sake of others. In prison, this ministry includes accepting some manipulation in order to accomplish a higher purpose.

In the final analysis, successful ministry comes when, in love, we dispense the grace that has been given to us. Like our Lord's ministry, we give this grace freely and expect nothing in return. The response to our gift of grace does not determine successful ministry; rather, it is determined by the spirit in which it is offered. Such ministry relates to attitudes of the heart that no person can judge; therefore, it is in God's realm.

It is easy for prison chaplains to become fatalistic, believing that it is impossible for them to make a difference. This attitude leads to apathy and loss of motivation. A realistic view of personal and institutional limitations is equally important, and so we must continue to prayerfully examine our actions, allowing the Spirit to search out all unrighteousness. Success in ministry is living the combined life of both servant and shepherd. In essence, we must reach out in sensitivity, compassion, and leadership. We must be all that we can for almighty God.

Areas of Focus for Inmates

The rest of chapter 1 outlines subjects that prison chaplains should emphasize in their ministry. The following areas are crucial to a prisoner's total development, and I have found that they are seldom integrated into Christian education.

Honesty

It is imperative that chaplains and other leaders impress upon offenders the need to be honest before God. Prisoners should be honest not only about their sins but also about their feelings. Being honest about our emotions requires continuous self-examination, without which there is little possibility of significant growth. Inmates who are in a state of denial for legal or other reasons cannot receive divine grace. Only an honest heart permits repentance and daily renewal.

Although most felons experience guilt, many of them find it too painful to talk about their crimes—both in therapy and in prayer. The church needs to be sensitive to this pain, helping inmates to search out the dark corners of their lives and encouraging them to share their findings with God.

Discipline

Some people find it hard to use the word *discipline* when speaking about spiritual matters—spirituality is normally understood and conveyed in abstract ways. Moreover, because prison is already a highly structured place, felons tend to resist discipline when it comes to religious matters. Yet, the absence of discipline is what brings many individuals to prison, and it also prevents them from moving beyond the basics of their faith.

Without structure, controls, and limitations, life becomes distorted and unbalanced. Only discipline permits the spiritual nurturing that transforms people. Meditation, prayer, study, and worship become superficial or nonexistent activities when there is no time allotted for them. Inmates need to know that discipline is essential for all aspects of life, including their spirituality.

Behavior modification is important to discipline, but it is seldom taught in the church because of its humanistic roots—it is based on reason rather than emotion. Modifying our behavior involves practicing positive responses to situations. We must recognize that negative reactions only heighten problems, while positive behavior brings beneficial results. Behavior modification has continuing effects, because it recycles as inmates become reinforced through positive feedback.

Some people think that modifying their behavior is false and manipulative, primarily because their real feelings are held in check. While this statement has some validity, the principal concern in prison is to prevent relational conflict. Therefore, behavior modification is important for everyone, particularly those imprisoned for uncontrolled behavior. The church can be instrumental in teaching this discipline by offering biblical examples of eliminating negative interactions.

Objectivity

The prejudices of prisoners prevent the objectivity that makes maturity possible. There can be many reasons for an inmate's narrow and distorted vision. Among the most common influences are a lack of education and travel, strong cultural and ethnic beliefs, peer pressure, past lifestyles, and lack of work experience.

Narrow-mindedness in the church is usually a result of religious legalism and intolerance. This attitude causes critical and judgmental behavior that can generate turmoil and division. Rigidity is a highly visible problem in penal congregations, and it lacks an easy solution. Nevertheless, the church must continue to do its part to improve relationships between people with different beliefs and help stimulate personal growth. Chaplains can accomplish this goal, in part, by affirming sensitivity in their teaching.

Developing objectivity can be laborious because it encompasses many conflicting emotions. The path to new understandings is difficult, but the journey is worth it. Teaching prison congregations the concept and practice of objectivity is imperative, for it relates to faith and the teachings of Christ—mutual healing, unity, and evangelistic outreach.

Realistic Expectations

Prisoners with unrealistic expectations set themselves up for disappointment, anger, and depression. When we reflect on the needs of inmates, we understand why they look to others for encouragement and support. However, prisoners are inclined to expect too much from other people, which can ultimately cause distress. In the isolated world of incarceration prisoners lose much of their perspective. They focus on themselves and frequently fail to understand the feelings, limitations, and problems of other people. The incarcerated tend to have unrealistic expectations of family members, friends, government agencies, and institutions.

Although the church represents hope for offenders, some penal residents attend religious services for the wrong reasons—possibly to influence prison staff members or parole boards to act on their behalf. The attendance of these individuals is usually short-lived when their expectations are not satisfied. Yet, felons can be led toward realistic goals and expectations, with the church serving as guide and supporter.

Understanding Change

Most people view change with some trepidation. Contemplating the unknown brings uncomfortable thoughts and emotions, and some-times prisoners' concerns are justified. Although change is a natural and necessary part of life, some transitions are extremely difficult. Incarceration can be placed in this category because prisoners expe-rience loss and degradation on a daily basis.

Few offenders understand change as something positive, and the church seldom addresses this subject. While inner transformation is emphasized, situational and other types of change are not discussed. Yet, because change is unavoidable, it should be examined in the context of the Scriptures and Christian living—it teaches us patience, tolerance, and perseverance, and it enables us to serve others. Understanding change is crucial for inmates, all of whom live in the midst of extreme instability.

The Positive Aspects of Incarceration

Because many negative images surround imprisonment, fatalism seems to overshadow rehabilitative efforts. Yet, incarceration has a positive side. Although offenders are distressed by their prison sen-tences, some of them firmly believe that their forced removal from society has given them a second chance.

A number of felons feel that their incarceration literally saved them because their luck was running out. In the outside world they lived a life controlled by drugs, crime, and violence. While these prisoners did not actually desire incarceration, they now realize that "getting caught" saved them from self-destruction. For these individ-uals imprisonment is truly an agent for change.

Inmates also talk about the people they have hurt, specifically family members and friends who are traumatized by the inmate's lifestyle and prison sentence. This damage certainly leaves scars, but incarceration can also bring hope to everyone involved. Because the criminal's damaging activities are terminated, restored relationships and new beginnings are possible. Yet even when relationships are beyond reconciliation, individual healing can take place.

The prison experience invites a transforming reflection. Inmates examine their lives within the framework of their relationships. They look at themselves through the eyes of other inmates. Living closely with their peers enables offenders to see themselves more clearly.

Many do not like what they see. Convicted criminals initiate their own rehabilitation. Peer insights are often the starting point for this process.

The Transforming Power of the Church

We must continuously strive to improve the conditions of our prisons and implement worthwhile programs. To do so the philosophy of corrections must change, and qualified and trained staff members must be hired in all departments. In addition to fulfilling stringent employment requirements, all prison staff should receive ongoing education in the social sciences. An understanding of human relationships is necessary for both treatment and security personnel.

The church should be an example and promoter of education, with prison clergy serving as resource people. Pastors are trained in the social sciences. Consequently, correctional employees can benefit from their knowledge and vast experiences. Unfortunately, some prison administrators fail to recognize the education and skills of chaplains, which is a tremendous loss to a system with so many needs.

While chaplains can be good resources for prison staff, the primary mission of the church is to transform lives. Through a concerned and compassionate presence, Christian ministry draws inmates to the message of redemption. Without forgiveness and the chance for a new life, prisoners have little initiative to move in a positive direction. The gospel of Jesus Christ and the encouragement of the church brings hope to countless inmates. Some prison employees may deny the power of the church to transform, but it remains the claim of offenders whose lives manifest this truth.

Prisoners need to know that there is total forgiveness through the atonement of Christ, regardless of their past. The church must also show them how their past can be utilized for God's glory. Their past sins and present forgiveness, combined with the trials of incarceration, enable them to show compassion toward others—a compassion that begins in prison and accomplishes God's will through a developing priesthood.

A particular inmate comes to mind. This individual approached me after a worship service, stating that he was full of bitterness and anger. He was concerned that he would be released to society with these feelings still intact. He confessed that he had wanted to talk to me many times, but he felt that it was not the "manly" thing to do. However, with his parole plan finally approved, he needed to share his feelings. This young man informed me that he wanted the inner peace that he saw in Christian inmates. He was astounded that prisoners could actually possess contentment. I assured him that the peace he saw was real and that he also could receive it.

This story is a clear example of how God works in our penal institutions. It exemplifies the witness of Christian inmates and their influence on other residents. It also reveals that regardless of circumstances, God's plan for us begins at the time of our conversion. Prisons are mission fields that desperately need a strong priesthood, and the most effective servants are the incarcerated.

2

Inmate Stressors

Research Data on Stress

Medical research indicates that stress can affect the circulatory system, digestive tract, lungs, muscles, and joints. It may also cause psychosomatic illnesses and emotional disorders. Stress can even affect spiritual growth because those who are consumed by tension often become defensive and hostile, which can block overall development (McQuade and Aikman 1974, 20–124).

Thomas H. Holmes and R. H. Rahe, professors of psychiatry at the University of Washington, developed a stress scale of common life experiences. At the top of their scale they assigned a stress value of 100 to the death of a spouse. They then assigned stress values to other events of change and loss in the lives of the people they studied. Holmes and Rahe discovered that approximately 50 percent of the persons with a cumulative stress value between 150 and 299 (within one year) developed some type of illness (Clinebell 1984, 188).

The following Social Readjustment Scale reflects their research (ibid., 189–90):

Life Event	Stress Value
1. Death of spouse	100
2. Divorce	73
3. Marital separation	65
4. Detention (jail or other)	63
5. Death of a close family member	63
6. Major personal injury or illness	53
7. Marriage	50
8. Fired from work	47
9. Marital reconciliation	45
10. Retirement	45
11. Major change in health/behavior of family member	44
12. Pregnancy	40
13. Sexual difficulties	39
14. New family member (birth, adoption)	39
15. Major business readjustment	39
16. Major financial change	38
17. Death of a close friend	37
18. Changing to a different type of work	36
19. Major change in number of arguments with spouse	35
20. Mortgage or major loan	31
21. Foreclosure on mortgage loan	30
22. Major change in employment responsibilities	29
23. Son or daughter leaving home	29
24. Trouble with in-laws	29
25. Outstanding personal achievement	28
26. Spouse beginning or terminating employment	26
27. Beginning or ceasing formal education	26
28. Major change in living conditions	25
29. Revision of personal habits	24
30. Trouble with work supervisor	23
31. Major change in working hours or conditions	20

32.	Change in residence	20
33.	Changing to a new school	20
34.	Major change in type or amount of recreation	19
35.	Major change in church activities	19
36.	Major change in social activities	18
37.	Loan (not a major item)	17
38.	Major change in sleeping habits	16
39.	Major change in number of family gatherings	15
40.	Major change in eating habits	15
41.	Vacations	13
42.	Christmas	12
43.	Minor violations of the law	11

Many life stressors are not included in this scale, for example, poverty, sexism, environmental problems, racism, or anxieties and fears resulting from personal trauma. Also, while detention is mentioned, long prison sentences are not considered in the ratings (Clinebell 1984, 190).

The chart developed by Holmes and Rahe provides guidelines and insights into stress, but it does not begin to address the multiple stress factors related to imprisonment. Incarceration includes many of the stressors found on the scale, but the extreme loss and environmental tensions experienced by inmates heightens each stressor.

Diagnostic Reporting

In the evaluation and reporting of stress factors, clinicians use the Psychosocial Stressor Scale as a guideline. This scale is found in the *Diagnostic and Statistical Manual of Mental Disorders*, or the *DSM-III-R* (see Williams 1987). When evaluating a person, a therapist indicates that stressors are either *predominantly acute* (less than six months) or *enduring* (greater than six months). These two categories are based on a scale that ranges from zero to six, with the latter representing a catastrophic situation (ibid., 20, 21, 34, 35). This method of evaluating and reporting stress has some complex facets. It is mentioned in its simplest form here to show that health professionals take stress seriously. Stress that lasts more than six months is considered an enduring situation, which obviously applies to most individuals who are incarcerated.

The Global Assessment of Functioning Scale (GAF) is also found in the *DSM-III-R*. The GAF scale reflects *noticed symptoms* in the form of psychological, social, and occupational functioning related to mental health. This scale permits the clinician to indicate his or her overall judgment of a person's mental health through the use of a number code that represents symptoms ranging from *absent or minimal* to *persistent danger of severely injuring oneself or others*. The scale does not include impairment in functioning caused by environmental issues, which is important in the evaluation of prisoners (ibid., 22, 23, 37). Clearly, the multiple and accumulative stressors of prison life cannot be adequately measured.

Stress and Burnout

The psychologist Herbert Freudenberger coined the word *burnout*, which is commonly understood as depression following continued stress (Minirth et al. 1986, 14). Freudenberger defines burnout in the following way:

> Burnout is the loss of enthusiasm, energy, idealism, perspective, and purpose. It can be viewed as a state of mental, physical, and spiritual exhaustion brought on by continued stress. . . . Too much stress, without learning and applying certain coping techniques, can lead to clinical depression (ibid., 15).

Depression is evident in correctional facilities, often destroying inmate advancements and potential. Having lost their enthusiasm, perspective, and hope, some felons withdraw into their own world of cynicism. Anger and aggressive behavior also indicates chronic depression. These moods affect the entire institution, leaving the lingering possibility for conflict.

Specific Areas of Inmate Stress

The first part of this chapter provided a brief explanation of the complexities of stress and how they can affect a person's total being. This basic knowledge is a helpful introduction to the specific areas of inmate stress that we will now examine.

Convicted criminals enter penal institutions faced with the trauma of arrest, financial loss, and family pressures, which are aggravated by an apathetic, demoralizing, and dangerous prison environment. Trying to cope in the harsh physical conditions of prison, inmates find that they are alone in their often severe struggles. Prisoners are plagued by relentless stress, and they lack the resources and support that are available to other members of society.

Prison communities are similar in many ways to free society. In fact, they reflect our world, sharing many of the same problems, such as the strive for self-worth, gratification, and recognition. In prison, as in free society, there are clashes for power and control in which the strong abuse the weak.

However, because of the multiplicity of personal and institutional dynamics, prisons remain unique and complex communities. Individuals of diverse backgrounds are forced to coexist in confined quarters for the contradictory goals of punishment and rehabilitation, and every conceivable form of interaction is found. In prison, we find those who have gone to negative extremes in society seeking to be understood in a place that has little capacity or empathy to respond. Prisons unquestionably need order, and yet, by their very nature they threaten all order. In essence, they are societies of pain, confusion, and anger.

Correctional facilities are molded by the clashes of races, cultures, and religions, where prisoners compete for power, control, and survival. They are neighborhoods of discontent where anxiety and fear translate into mistrust and manipulation. As communities separated from society, prisons function apart from the rapidly changing world, and this environment affects tension levels. A prisoner's socialization terminates when he or she enters prison. This abrupt interruption of life, and the loss of support systems that comes with it, are emotionally devastating.

While institutional structures and rules are necessary, they foster negative attitudes and increase population stress. Inmates complain that some of the rules, for example those related to incoming mail and dress codes, are overbearing and have nothing to do with safety and security. Many felons believe that the enforcement of unnecessary regulations destroys the little dignity they still possess.

Most offenders come from lower socioeconomic segments of society, and they enter the system with numerous problems, such as fractured relationships and chronic poverty. Since their previous way of life failed, they begin their prison sentence in a defeated emotional state and, therefore, can become dangerous. In his book on deviant behavior, David Matza writes, "When the conventional rules and roles that organize social life and bind us to it are rendered inoperative, man appears dangerous and unrestrained" (1969, 45).

Others who have studied prisoners from the lower classes of society report similar findings. John Irwin reports that

> For lower class men, life is almost totally unpredictable. If they have sought stability at all, it has slipped from their grasp so quickly, so often and consistently, that they no longer pursue it. From childhood on, their only real gratification comes from action-seeking. . . . This directly relates to "manhood" or "machismo" (1970, 30).

The foregoing observations are apparent in our prisons. The power images communicated by many inmates are a manifestation of how they approach life. Prisoners try to hide their anxieties, insecurities, and fears through different types of role play, and machismo is one of them. Inmates may intimidate others by taking advantage of their physical appearance or by making verbal or written threats. Survival is the biggest concern in prison, and inmates actively seek ways to protect themselves. Some prisoners even project a false insanity or claim to have a communicable disease in order to keep abusive peers at a distance.

Incarceration is a continuing hardship and, while it may afford an opportunity for personal change, the ongoing crises associated with imprisonment are difficult to work through. Gary Collins offers the following observations:

> A crisis is a danger because it threatens to overwhelm the person or persons involved. Crises involve the loss of someone or something significant, a sudden shift in one's role or status, or the appearance of new and threatening people or events. Because the crisis situation is so intense and unique, we discover that our customary ways of handling stress and solving problems no longer work. This leads to a period of confusion and bewilderment, often accompanied by inefficient behavior and emotional upsets, including anxiety and discouragement, sorrow or guilt (1980, 48).

Collins's insights are significant when we consider the backgrounds, transitions, and environmental tensions of the incarcerated. Not only are crises magnified in prison, but the stress they create cannot adequately be processed. Because there is no outlet for their stress, prisoners become frustrated, and their actions unpredictable.

Abraham Maslow developed the theory that human motives must be satisfied at one level before the motives at the next level can direct and control behavior. His findings qualify as both a theory of personality and a theory of motivation. He illustrates his theory in a pyramid of human motives: basic biological needs are found at the bottom of the hierarchy, more complicated psychological motives are in the center, and *self-actualization,* or an acceptance of self, others, and reality, is at the top. In essence, with self-actualization we experience peace with ourselves and the created order (Houston et al. 1979, 296–97).

The following delineation reflects the primary concepts of Maslow's theory (Wilson 1976, 43). The particular categories, although general in nature, provide knowledge of human functioning that is helpful when studying prison communities.

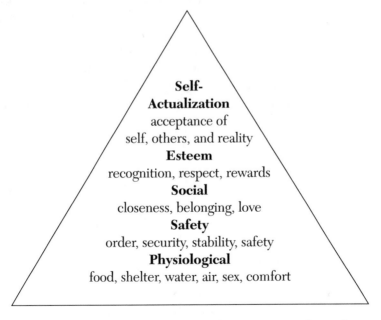

Self-
Actualization
acceptance of
self, others, and reality
Esteem
recognition, respect, rewards
Social
closeness, belonging, love
Safety
order, security, stability, safety
Physiological
food, shelter, water, air, sex, comfort

Numerous problems block motivation in correctional populations. Imprisonment places individuals in a "survival mode" and even when they advance personally, prisoners must exert great concentration to satisfy their basic needs and concerns. Felons expend most of their energy just trying to cope with the daily stress of incarceration. They struggle intensely to improve themselves in the midst of so many obstacles. They try to live "one day at a time," meaning that they must confront basic need issues each day.

An analysis of inmate stress, in view of Maslow's pyramid of motives, shows a bleak picture. Incarceration heightens existing tensions, removes motivation, destroys self-esteem, and promotes defensive attitudes and behavior. These are difficult obstructions for offenders to overcome as they attempt to improve their lives.

The remainder of this chapter discusses specific areas of inmate stress that present strong obstacles to personal development. It is important to remember that the nature of incarceration complicates and magnifies all stress.

Socialization

When individuals enter prison, their lives come to a sudden halt. The activities and friendships that were part of their daily living are replaced by an isolated world that is full of uncertainty and gripped by social stagnation. Imprisonment means living in a community that is frozen in time and space, where an offender's prior life becomes the primary source for understanding his or her surroundings. The incarcerated have knowledge of outside events and changes, but their inability to participate in them is stressful. They are cast into a world with different rules, where distortions and contradictions are the norm. For this reason, it is difficult for them to maintain perspective in the present. Because prisoners tend to live in the past, they do not mature socially.

Penal residents often talk about situations that occurred years ago as if they took place yesterday. Although nostalgia is common to everyone, some convicted felons are unable to acknowledge or accept changes that transpire while they are in prison. One obvious reason for their denial is the guilt and pain that these changes bring. Although this type of defense mechanism may relieve some immediate discomfort, it blocks the path to healing and personal growth. A continued state of social stagnation may even have irreversible effects.

Loss of Free Will and Control

Imprisonment makes inmates realize that free will is a precious gift. It is hard for us to imagine the accumulative loss of arrest and incarceration. For many people, the loss of freedom, even for brief periods, creates feelings of anxiety. When we view this in the context of a long prison sentence, we begin to understand a prisoner's emotional wounding. Prolonged imprisonment brings a sense of helplessness, invalidating the inmate's voice concerning personal and family matters.

Prisoners quickly learn that their influence and control is eroded on every level. While they expect this situation in a penal setting, they initially give little thought to how incarceration will affect their outside relationships. It is difficult for inmates to believe that supportive friends and relatives can become distant, independent, or even hostile. Because life in prison revolves around their own needs, they fail to understand how their incarceration affects others.

In my conversations with the incarcerated I have repeatedly heard cries of helplessness on issues related to the family. One inmate summed up his emotions by saying, "Incarceration is like being tied up and dropped into the sea. That's how much influence and control you have on the outside." Inmates experience confusion and despair as they begin to lose grip on the world they once influenced, often the most trying battle for the incarcerated. They only find resolve when they employ coping techniques and make adjustments. In an attempt to regain control and reduce tension and pain, some penal residents terminate all contact with the outside world. This is a painful decision, but desperation sometimes leads to drastic measures.

Incarceration quenches an individual's ability to make decisions in every area of daily life, from the choice of clothing and food to deciding whom to live with. Pleasures that were previously taken for granted, such as experiencing nature and travel, interchange with children, intimate relationships, and social events, are also taken away. With the passing of time, these aspects of freedom become sacred thoughts to prisoners. The unconscious decisions and mobility known to other people are replaced with manifold rules and an inflexible structure. Only when our free will is taken from us do we realize its importance.

From early morning until evening an inmate's movements are restricted and controlled by security dictates. Prison life is mechanical and removes any sense of individuality and personhood. Inmates are reduced to a dependent existence in which expression is discouraged, and sometimes those who voice their opinions are subject to psychological punishment. To survive and advance toward parole inmates must assume a passive and submissive role. Being vocal, even when it is justified, exposes them to institutional labels and setbacks.

Negative responses from staff may also surface if a resident exhibits special talent. Prison employees often interpret these talents as attempts to gain personal elevation and control, neither of which coincide with the prison philosophy of punishment. I have known felons who simply desired to use their skills as a means of giving something back to society. Their efforts, however, were terminated by staff members who insisted these prisoners had ulterior motives. Not allowing inmates to express themselves may satisfy the advocates of warehousing and punishment, but it only increases negativity and tension.

While prisoners should not be allowed to experience the freedom they had in the outside world, we must realize that everyone needs to engage in some manner of decision making, regardless of their situation. The idea that prisons are for punishment only reflects an ignorant and archaic approach to corrections that returns unchanged people to society. Some offenders actually leave prison worse than when they entered—for example, young inmates who are forced to live with seasoned criminals. Although we cannot blame the correctional system for everything, a number of institutional factors compound the problems that already exist.

Many prisoners have shared their frustrations and anger with me. One inmate disclosed rage toward a system that refused to recognize him as a human being with feelings and needs. He confessed that he feared how his anger would be ventilated if he were given freedom. This individual was certainly not guiltless, but much of what he expressed echoes the feelings of his peers.

We cannot forget that a prisoner's loss of freedom is his or her punishment, and anything more violates human rights. Prisons should try to change lives through techniques that direct inmate energy toward productive ends and improve self-esteem by encouraging offenders to change their attitudes and begin a new life. The objective of prisons should be to prepare residents for productive lives that begin within the institution. Positive results can come through incentives, pertinent programs, and concerned staff.

Low Self-Esteem

In her discourse "The Church as a Support to Families Under Stress," Sharon Telleen states that "self-esteem is essential in coping with stress. Labeling and placing someone in a dependency position where he or she cannot reciprocate will not enhance self-esteem. Individuals in a crisis need a feeling of pride, autonomy, and the respect of others if they are to effectively cope" (1980, 104). This statement was probably written without incarceration in mind, but its greater truth provides insights into the prison system. When the philosophy of corrections is punishment, little opportunity exists for inmates to build self-esteem. This attitude, in turn, affects coping abilities, tension levels, and rehabilitation.

Prisoners endure both real and imagined degradation, with extensive personal loss and failure resulting in an emotional quandary. Their anxiety is heightened by an unfeeling institution in which felons are categorized and identified by numbers. This damage to self-esteem has lasting effects. The poor self-concept and stigma of being a convicted felon is not something inmates can easily work through; it has a continuing impact on their lives.

The incarcerated seek identity and recognition in an indifferent environment. The penal system is simply not structured or motivated to treat inmates in a caring and personal way. Staff attitudes can sometimes be traced to inmate manipulation, but the prevailing reason for employee apathy and antagonism is that prisons have throughout history placed punishment before rehabilitation. Many people associated with correctional systems would argue against this statement by pointing to educational and therapeutic programs, but the personal deflation built into our prisons is evident to any reasonable observer.

Inmates justifiably believe that their legally imposed sentence is punishment enough and that additional degradation is abuse. But felons who file grievances or lawsuits become marked individuals who are viewed by staff as a threat. Prison employees rally to the support of fellow workers who are accused of abusive acts. Security personnel are particularly loyal to one another, which can spell disaster for a prisoner.

In his book *Power and Innocence,* Rollo May tells us that "man becomes a self only to the extent that he can know it, affirm it, and assert it" (1972, 141). His statement points out that our self-concept is based on how others perceive us, and it improves when there is positive feedback. Similarly, positive responses help us view others in a positive way.

Those who make educational, spiritual, vocational, and other advancements in prison improve their self-concept, which results in changed attitudes and behavior. Residents who improve themselves become more objective and tolerant. They exhibit a contentment and hope that is not seen in other inmates. With encouragement and direction, residents are better able to understand their past and what must be accomplished to improve their future.

Many individuals are incarcerated for acts that they committed to defend their self-image, reputation, honor, or understood rights. Their perception that these things were threatened may have been distorted, but the threat was very real to them at the time. Every person feels the need for self-worth and respect, including those who have violated the law. Regardless of their crimes, even the worst criminals deserve respect. Such an attitude is too much for some people to digest, including many correctional employees.

When prisoners cannot gain the respect they desire, they usually respond negatively to their environment in an attempt to combat frustration and pain or to regain control and dignity. The trauma caused by dehumanization is inevitably ventilated, and in prison the potential is explosive. Unfortunately, this danger is often disregarded by prison officials and employees.

The degrading conditions in prison serve as a constant reminder of an inmate's crimes and fall from grace. This attack to self-esteem tends to suppress any developing ego. In society one can find ways to avoid character threats. In prison it is impossible (Goffman 1967, 5). In an essay titled "The Inmate Social System," Gresham Sykes and Sheldon Messinger provide helpful insights concerning self-image:

> It is of greatest importance that the rigors imposed on the inmate by the prison officials do not represent relatively minor irritants which he can somehow endure; instead, the conditions of custody involve profound attacks on the prisoner's self-esteem or sense of personal worth, and these psychological pains may be far more threatening than physical maltreatment. . . . The isolation of the prisoner from the free community means that he has been rejected by society. . . . This rejection is understood by his uniform and the degradation of no longer having a name but a number. . . . It should be remembered that the offender has been drawn from society in which personal possessions and material achievement are closely linked with concepts of personal worth by numerous cultural definitions. In prison, however, the inmate finds himself reduced to a level of living near bare subsistence, and whatever physical discomforts his deprivation may entail, it apparently has deeper psychological signifi-

cance as a basic attack on the prisoner's conception of his own personal adequacy. . . . No less important, perhaps, is the ego threat that is created by the deprivation of heterosexual relationships. In the tense atmosphere of prison, with its perversions and constant references to the problems of sexual frustration, even those inmates who do not engage in overt homosexuality suffer acute attacks of anxiety about their masculinity (1960, 13–14).

Although correctional institutions strive for inmate advancement, psychological and emotional forms of punishment are firmly in place. Offenders live with the ambivalence of seeking achievement and simultaneously being reminded of their worthlessness. As a result, many residents become discouraged and do not engage in self-improvement programs. The incarcerated are not easily motivated, and any obstacle adds to the problem.

Often, inmates compensate for feelings of inferiority with hostility, because hating others seems better than destroying themselves. Without intervention, insecurities become more pronounced and destructive—especially when we consider the collective force of these emotions in a large institution. Some subcultures encourage their members to believe that hostility and the use of force are "manly" qualities. Consequently, immature personalities sometimes employ violence to compensate for feelings of inadequacy. Therefore, one solution to tension and violence is to help felons develop their potential and self-worth (Ellis 1977, 203–4).

Most prison assaults are rooted in poor self-esteem. After a particular violent assault, the assailant told me that he would do anything to get broad media attention. He admitted that he was craving recognition and was willing to kill or even give his own life for a fleeting moment of glory. While perhaps an extreme example, other prisoners have reached similar breaking points. Many inmates walk an emotional tightrope, particularly those with long prison sentences and those who receive frequent setbacks.

Insecurity leads felons to engage in different types of role play to intimidate their peers. They hope to prevent threats and confrontations by sending a message that others should keep their distance. For the same reason, some offenders join groups. Because there is more intimidation and protection in numbers, group affiliations are desirable and even perceived as necessary by some residents. Group membership can be based on culture, nationality, religion, race, criminal activity, or a common cause. A combination of these factors often determines group activity. Some groups are recognized communities within the institution, and so affiliation with prison groups also brings identification, recognition, and power. These are important elements for individuals who are living with extreme loss.

Because most prisoners return to society and rehabilitating them is an objective of the correctional system, it makes sense to establish an environment that will enhance their self-worth and improve their philosophy of life. But society must desire to change the system and admit that the old methods have not worked. Improving corrections necessitates political decisions, finances, and the determination to stay the course. Moreover, our prisons need educated and compassionate staff members who will commit themselves to the concepts of rehabilitation. Too many problems in our current system have developed because of insensitive, ignorant, and apathetic prison staff.

Dehumanization and punishment are inconsistent with divine forgiveness and grace. Therefore, it is hard for convicted criminals to internalize and live the teachings of the church. Prison chaplains must be cognizant of this and respond by developing themes and methods of ministry to penetrate these obstacles. But all prison staff members should be concerned with the transformation of offenders, which means that they need to be sensitive to the emotional state and needs of inmates.

Relational Loss

Men and women who enter prison are separated from their social world. Regardless of how fragmented that world was, it still gave them a sense of identity and belonging. When we evaluate a prisoner's past environment negatively, it only exacerbates their loss. The incarcerated live in the destructiveness of their past lives, which includes damaged relationships. Family members and friends struggle with the way their own lives have changed with a loved one in prison. Inmates who seek understanding and support from them may feel neglected.

Family members often react to incarceration with shock, confusion, anger, or embarrassment. They must deal with peer pressure, new dependencies, changed roles and structures, and financial troubles, along with feelings of abandonment, loneliness, guilt, insecurity, and uncertainty. In addition, family conflicts, such as discipline problems with children and the stress of one-parent families, revolve around the incarcerated person. The family finds its world being pulled in many directions. Like the inmate, family members are also reduced to a "survival mode" that threatens relationships and order.

To endure their hardship, families move through a necessary process of independence from prisoners. Even family members that maintain contact with inmates experience degrees of emotional separation, especially evident when an individual is released from prison. Regardless of how much contact a prisoner has had with loved ones, months or years of imprisonment change relationships.

Offenders who separate themselves from outside matters become better adjusted to prison life. They cannot live in two worlds and maintain emotional stability. Prisoners who become consumed in family affairs that they cannot control quickly feel the increased tension. Certain areas of responsibility must be relinquished to others. Being in prison is stressful enough without added outside pressures.

Relational loss sometimes leads inmates to employ coping mechanisms, such as denial and fantasy. I will never forget one young man who often went to extremes in an attempt to fill a relational void. He had no immediate family or close friends, and his distant relatives terminated all communications after his arrest. This individual had a dependent personality and was constantly in need of recognition and assurance. One afternoon he walked into my office with a very large handmade birthday card. He said that he received the card from very close friends, emphasizing that they always remember him on special days. My response to him was encouraging, but I doubted the veracity of his story. I later learned that this troubled individual had spent hours making the birthday card, after which he mailed it to himself.

I have counseled many convicted criminals whose accumulated loss seemed beyond the limits of emotional control. Chaplains at large institutions continuously counsel inmates who have experienced loss through divorce, broken family relationships, and deaths. At Rockview, some of the most feared prisoners wept in the privacy of my office as they learned of a family illness or death.

Imprisonment prevents participation in meaningful family events, such as holidays, births, weddings, deaths, graduations, religious functions, and other celebrations. Reflection on these important and enjoyable times keeps felons living in the past. The problem, however, is that their families are coping with the harsh realities of the present. These tensions seem impossible to resolve.

Separation is most difficult when there are emergencies at home, including serious accidents, illnesses, or deaths. Some inmates experience multiple family deaths during their incarceration, and they must often grieve alone. Prisoners who are unable to attend funerals for financial, geographical, or security reasons experience feelings of intense guilt, isolation, and helplessness. Their inability to say good-bye to a loved one leaves open wounds. Prisoners who cannot attend funeral services sometimes ask the family for photographs of the deceased person in the casket. These pictures may be the only pictures the inmate has of the person.

During my ministry at Rockview I met one prisoner whose mother and three-year-old daughter were dying at the same time. In another case, a resident had three tragedies in one week—his son sustained a fatal gunshot wound, his father had a stroke, and his mother died. While these are certainly unusual situations, numerous prisoners find themselves confronted with ongoing loss. The longer their prison sentence, the more likely they are to experience this kind of trauma.

A large percentage of prisoners come from inner-city environments that are entrenched in poverty and crime. Many of these individuals experience multiple losses while they are incarcerated because it is common for them to have family members who are involved in crime. I have talked to residents who told me that most of their male family members were incarcerated. Because of their surroundings and lifestyles, these same families often become victims of crime, including serious assaults and homicides. Narcotics are frequently involved. A number of prisoners have been called to my office because someone in their family died of a drug overdose or was a homicide victim.

Through counseling sessions, chaplains see a side of inmates that is not visible to other staff members. Prison clergy hear the remorse and desperation of distraught individuals. They also listen to inmates who admit to disorders that resist treatment. Chaplains see past the anger and machismo, and they often become the recipients of an inmate's innermost feelings and thoughts. Through intimate conversation, they witness the suffering that results from personal loss.

In the midst of this loss and pain, offenders labor to understand how their imprisonment affects others. Although they are concerned for their families and friends, sensitivity toward others is overshadowed by their own needs. In fact, many offenders have unrealistic expectations, and they impose strong demands, forgetting that loved ones also are struggling to work through their own issues.

It is normal for prisoners to be abrasive with parents, spouses, and friends when they do not respond to their desires, one of which may be financial support. But in most cases, these same family members and friends are already supporting the inmate's children. The prisoner's high expectations and constant demands trigger increased frustration and anger from families, which, in turn, comes back to the inmate.

The inmate's parents live with intense sorrow and stress. In many instances, they are the only ones who remain faithful to the offender. But there are parents who, after years of helping a child, finally withdraw to protect themselves. Over the years I have spoken to parents who spent thousands of dollars on legal fees, even to the point of selling their homes and other valuable possessions, only to be continuously disappointed by the inmate.

Many of the dynamics in relationships between prisoners and their families also exist between inmates and their friends. Some people have difficulty relating to a friend who has been incarcerated, especially if he or she was convicted of crimes that involve sex or extreme violence. Friends may feel uncomfortable with the criminal element. Also, separation can decrease common interests and relational bonds.

Studies indicate that when religious beliefs are present, there is more mutual support during periods of separation. H. McCubbin studied the coping responses of families experiencing separation in one of three conditions: regular, one-week separation related to employment (minimal stress); regular, eight-month separation for naval sea duty (moderate stress); and separation of six years for families of prisoners of war or soldiers missing in action (severe stress) (Telleen 1980, 96–97).

The families who participated in McCubbin's study reported that religious belief was an important factor in their ability to manage the tensions of separation, particularly for those experiencing moderate and severe stress. Spiritual support helps maintain the family unit, contributes to individual self-esteem through love and care, and serves as a reference point for norms, values, and expectations that can guide families in stressful situations. Similarly, when all family members believe in God they form a bond of trust with each other (ibid.).

There is no scientific data relating to separations caused by imprisonment, but everything I have seen as a prison chaplain supports the foregoing conclusions. It cannot be said that religion alone holds families together or that spiritual people do not terminate relationships. Nevertheless, there is a closer bond and more "staying power" between people who share a common faith. The testimony of numerous inmates and their families reinforces this truth.

Regarding the stress that accompanies separation, McCubbin found that the following coping strategies were common to all the families in the study: (1) establishing independence; and (2) increasing self-sufficiency. In many instances spouses learned to manage finances and worked to attain the skills needed to manage a family alone (ibid., 97–98).

While these are necessary survival mechanisms for the family, prisoners feel increased anxiety when family independence is evident. They already feel isolated and emotionally dependent. *Social support* may be defined as support that is accessible to an individual through ties to other persons, groups, and the larger community (Telleen 1980, 98). Thus, the family unit and other outside relationships are extremely important to the incarcerated.

Research shows that family members are most helpful in long-term enduring crises, while friends are more helpful in acute short-term situations. In addition, people look first to their family for support before going to the community (ibid., 99). This is certainly true for prisoners.

Although members of the immediate family (mother, father, and children) generally live in separate and sometimes distant households from other relatives, they remain active participants in the primary family network. In other words, the family still functions as an extended unit (ibid.).

G. Caplan identifies nine ways in which a healthy family supports its members. This support also facilitates the emotional mastery and coping strategies that enable individuals to deal with stress (ibid., 99–100).

1. **The family as a collector and disseminator of information**
   Multigenerational learning is possible in both directions, from young to old and old to young.
2. **The family as a feedback guidance system**
   Family members can help one another make valid assessments of their behavior in new situations by giving their reactions.
3. **The family as a source of ideology**
   The family provides belief systems, value systems, and codes of

behavior that are expected of its members. These traditions offer a source of guidance and support during a crisis.

4. **The family as a guide and mediator in problem solving**
   Family members guide each other in dealing with problems and finding external sources of care and assistance.
5. **The family as a source of practical service and aid**
   Mutual aid among family members in the form of money, gifts, and help with household tasks is an important source of support during a crisis or periods of transition.
6. **The family as a haven for rest and recuperation**
   The family legitimizes the need for rest so that individuals have a chance to collect their thoughts in order to resume control of a crisis without feeling they have lost control while resting.
7. **The family as a reference and control group**
   As a reference group, the family does not judge. As a control group, it rewards success in adhering to the family code and punishes failure in full knowledge that the destinies of family members are bound together and that they will continue to accept one another for who they are.
8. **The family as a source and validator of identity**
   During a crisis of transition, an individual can become uncertain about his or her identity, strengths, and abilities. The family supports these individuals by reminding them of past and present successes.
9. **The family as a contributor to emotional mastery**
   The family can aid an individual in constructive problem solving and help the individual control feelings of despair and helplessness by their continual presence.

Caplan's data is based on healthy family units and seems more applicable to free members of society. But regardless of the circumstances, this information clearly shows the importance of the family as a support system in a time of crisis. Like other members of society, a large percentage of offenders come from fragmented and dysfunctional families. However, such conditions do not undermine the importance of the family unit.

The family serves as a source of identity, acceptance, validation, economic assistance, wisdom, and guidance. Family members aid in problem solving and affect emotional stability. One can imagine the deep loss that occurs when this support system is lost through incarceration. The loss becomes greater when prisoners experience deaths in the family. Some inmates feel that their arrest and incarceration contributed to the family member's death. In such cases, intense guilt often leads these offenders to communicate their own death wish as a form of punishment.

Some inmate families do not offer strong support systems, but prisoners still feel the loss when these relationships are severed. In spite of problems, families remain the roots, identity, and stabilizing force in the lives of many inmates. In some cases, a prisoner's relatives may be their only glimmer of hope. In my experience of counseling inmates after family deaths, I have repeatedly heard the question, "What do I have left? He or she was all I had on the outside—my only support." These words undoubtedly signal a critical time in an offender's life.

Personal Guilt

Most people believe that prisoners lack remorse for their crimes; however, the opposite is usually true. One reason for this misconception is the inmate denial that others perceive through superficial observations. There are degrees of denial in everyone, and inmates are no exception, but their remorse is difficult to detect for distinct reasons. For example, those continuing the legal process through appeals believe that any exposure of guilt can be detrimental to their pursuits. Felons also fear that the prejudices of staff members and other inmates may somehow be used against them. Depending on the circumstances and the stigma of his or her offense, an inmate's life could even be in danger.

Many inmates and staff members feel that crimes against children, especially sex crimes, are unforgivable offenses. For this reason, persons convicted of such abuses exercise great caution concerning their past. The idea that it is impossible to keep secrets in prison is certainly true, but these individuals make every effort to distance themselves from inquiries and aggression. If they are questioned about their crimes, they respond with emphatic denial.

Convicted law enforcement officers also maintain low visibility. Many offenders release their anger on these men and women merely because they were once part of the legal system. A number of offenders seek ways to ventilate their frustrations, and ex-police officers are perfect targets. To avoid anticipated problems, some institutions make special provisions for convicted officers. A detective I worked with was arrested for vehicular manslaughter and was sentenced to a county prison. Immediately after he was incarcerated his life was threatened by other inmates. Fortunately, prison officials took the threats seriously, and precautionary steps were taken.

Most convicted felons live with intense guilt. This guilt is reinforced by the physically and emotionally punishing environment of the penal system, and it continues when the person returns to society. The stigma of criminal conviction is a burden that prisoners carry throughout their lives, and nothing can remove it from their minds and consciences. To say that inmates do not live with guilt simply because they do not expose their crimes is a false conclusion. In reality, prisoners withhold their feelings because of possible retribution.

Living Conditions

It takes considerable time for criminals to accept the realities of imprisonment. The process begins with shock and disbelief and goes through many phases and adjustments. Those who continue to make legal appeals maintain hope, but few of these appeals succeed. When legal resources are depleted, acceptance becomes necessary for an inmate's emotional survival. Nevertheless, this acceptance does not eliminate their anger toward a system whose crowded and often inhumane conditions impinge upon basic needs and understood rights. The paramount problem for inmates is overcrowded living conditions. A study conducted by Paul Hopstock, John Aiello, and Andrew Baum shows that crowded conditions have adverse physical, mental, and social effects (1979, 11, 17–19). The following studies are also pertinent to prison conditions.

> D'Atri found heightened levels of systolic and diastolic blood pressures among inmates housed under conditions characterized by high social density, and Cox et al. reported heightened palmar sweat levels for prisoners of socially dense institutions (ibid., 11).

> Research conducted at Rutgers University by Aiello and Epsten during 1974 and 1975 reveals interesting data on long-term social density conditions. They studied dormitory life in which three students were assigned to quarters designed for two individuals. Their study concluded that such conditions create negative cognitive and affective reactions. . . . The suggestion is that long-term density conditions may produce stress related

physiological and psychological problems if adequate coping strategies are not found (ibid., 17–19).

Baum and Valins found that residents of dormitory environments characterized by high social density performed more poorly when solving anagrams alone than did residents of dormitories housing them in smaller groups (ibid., 11).

Research concerning the effects of residential density on responsiveness to the social environment is also relevant. Subjects experiencing high density conditions are more likely to withdraw from social interaction with strangers and to have problems relating to neighbors. Residents of high density environments were also less likely to engage in self-disclosure, form group consensus, and to help others. The general pattern of these results is that residents of high social density environments engage in withdrawal and decrease their level of social interaction (ibid.).

High social density in prison can produce negative emotional responses and a lessened tolerance for crowding. Tolerance for crowding decreases over time, which is counter to notions that people can easily adapt to crowded situations (Cox et al. 1979, 100–101).

These studies are significant when we consider how social density can affect penal residents. Moreover, some of these studies were conducted in positive settings where conditions were not extreme—they lacked the stress factors that are specific to incarceration.

Other studies indicate that there is seldom violence in minimum security institutions where individuals are treated in a more humane manner. Vernon Fox reports that "discipline in most prisons which experienced riots appears to have been on the side of rigidity" (1956, 41). Some people may counter these observations by pointing out that there are many different types of prisoners and circumstances, but we cannot doubt the danger of placing any personality type in overcrowded and inhumane environments.

One study involving a prison in Michigan provides five causes for a major disturbance. This study caught my attention because it took place in 1952, and yet the findings of the investigators have a contemporary sound to them (ibid., 304).

1. Excessive size of the prison system
2. Heterogeneous population
3. Overcrowded living conditions
4. Understaffing
5. Inadequate training for correctional officers

It is apparent that governments have learned few lessons over the years, because these same conditions exist in many institutions today. Overcrowding and inadequately trained employees are the most dangerous factors. Overcrowded prisons filled with troubled individuals are powder kegs, especially when employees lack interpersonal skills and pertinent training. More will be said about staff and inmate relationships later in this chapter.

Violence is more conspicuous in our society today because of an increase in the population and crowded living. These conditions exacerbate the aggravations and tensions that lead to anger and violence. Moreover, cultural differences, feelings of inadequacy, and economic problems also contribute to the increase in violence. The problems of violence in free society parallel those in prison populations.

Max Rosenbaum says the following about overcrowding and aggression:

> This density of living together, to which man is forced, comes to the point where he does not anymore have the freedom to put his aggressions into action or use them in a socially constructive way in free nature. He has to restrain himself constantly and to comply to the many others surrounding him. He is always reminded of the many social norms, so that the aggression is bottled up to the point where it bursts forth in destructive ways.
>
> As observations of group behavior of wild rats have shown, the reciprocal aggressions increased the denser the interactions of the rats became. Reciprocal intolerance was observed which drove the wild-living rats to the expulsion of others, particularly of their offspring. It became apparent in a mice experiment that the smaller the cage was, or the more mice that were forced to

interact because of lack of room, the more the aggression of
each animal increased (1983, 96).

Continuous restraint of feelings and emotions also leads to aggression. Except in therapeutic programs, positive behavior in prison is
understood as suppressed feelings. Those who openly express themselves to prison staff and peers are viewed as a threat. Inmates know
that negative behavior leaves a lasting blemish. Therefore, they work
hard at keeping their feelings under control. The problem, however,
is that bottled-up emotions are potentially explosive.

Milton Layden (1977, 222) tells us that the following circumstances lead to anger: a clear and precise danger to one's survival;
frustration of one's self-esteem; a threat to one's close personal relationships; and a threat to one's sense of belonging. Similarly, the
National Commission on Violence concludes that all people are likely
to aggress against others, because all people experience frustrations
of varying intensity during their lives (ibid.). The worse the frustration, the greater the readiness of aggression, and even violence.

These statements are shocking when we consider penal conditions. Living conditions vary from one facility to another, but older
prisons are obviously the worst. They have small, unsanitary cells
with poor lighting, ventilation, and heat control. Inmates must also
cope with the intense noise and foul odors that are common to many
prisons. Authorities on criminality and imprisonment point out that a
substandard environment and the scarcity of rehabilitation measures
not only cause institutional violence but also promote criminal activity when prisoners are released (ibid., 227).

In his book *Christian Counseling*, Gary Collins mentions the following aspects of environment that influence aggression. He explains
that our environment affects our moods, attitudes, and responses
(1980, 467–68).

1. Noise
Noise can increase tension and irritability, prevent sleep, inter-
fere with job performance, and cause loss of appetite.

2. Crowding
At times we all need a quiet place where we can withdraw for a
time of solitude. When such withdrawal is impossible, tensions
build, tempers flare, and we feel trapped.

3. Architecture

Room shape, colors, type and arrangement of furniture, decorations, temperature, and lighting all have psychological effects on people. Architecture and design have a subtle bearing on work productivity, interpersonal relations, attitudes, emotions, and the extent to which people feel comfortable and relaxed.

I have always been amazed at how even the smallest environmental improvements in prison can change attitudes and behavior. The positive results of these improvements make them worth the investment. Treating inmates with disdain will only solicit defensive reactions—a basic truth that some prison staff fail to grasp. Prison officials must work to rectify environmental problems, whether they need to improve poor living conditions or stop verbal antagonism by employees. Failure to respond to environmental complaints can be costly.

Some prisons house more than twice the population they can safely accommodate. This situation creates security and safety issues for both staff and inmates. Crowded cell blocks place offenders in a dangerous position should an emergency occur, such as fire, natural disaster, plant malfunction, or assaults and riots. Even if a riot can be contained to a particular cell block, the destructive potential of over-populated units is massive. At the Rockview facility there are almost five hundred prisoners in cell blocks that should hold only two hundred and fifty people. Another prison in Pennsylvania has residential units that house approximately seven hundred inmates where only half this number can live safely.

Crowded conditions often necessitate placing two prisoners in a cell that is unfit for even one person. This lack of privacy and emotional space is extremely stressful for prisoners, particularly if one or both of the individuals are consumed with personal problems. Yet, within these confined quarters felons must maintain good behavior or risk being cited for institutional misconducts, which often bring additional punishment.

Living with another prisoner in a small cell is one of the most frequent inmate complaints. Inmates approach chaplains daily, communicating frustrations and fears about their cell partners. Their concerns range from uncleanliness to theft and assault. Many offenders experience sleepless nights because of relational tensions with their cell mate. Some situations become so troublesome that residents refuse to enter their cells—they would rather be cited with misconduct and be sent to solitary confinement.

Although institutions do permit cell changes, administrators resist making these moves without proof of an assault or serious threat. Prison supervisors contend that relational tension is common, and it is impossible to respond to every inmate who experiences conflict. But some living arrangements are expecially volatile, and they should be investigated more thoroughly. It is inconceivable that convicted criminals, some of whom have severe emotional problems, can live together in small cells without repercussions. The cell arrangements that exist in many facilities can be compared to two individuals living in a locked bathroom. For instance, an average cell, which measures about eight square feet, contains two people, their personal belongings, a double bunk, a table, a small television, a sink, and an open toilet.

Space is not only a problem in cells and cell blocks, but in the entire prison compound. While some institutions have considerable acreage, prisoners have little space and mobility within the security area. This means that felons cannot find the solitude they need when tensions build. Even when they are alone in their cell, activity and noise is all around them. Prisoners feel anxiety just knowing that there is no place of refuge.

The exercise yards of some prisons are substantial in size, but they draw large crowds when the weather is clear. As these yards become full, it is not unusual for residents to confront one another over desired turf and available athletic equipment. The possibility of these dangers keeps some prisoners away from the yard.

Peer Interaction

Because of conflicting emotions and deep personal needs, honest and lasting relationships seldom develop in prison. When we consider the emotional turmoil in prison communities, we understand why there is relational strife. Inmates need recognition, as can be seen in the way they strive for attention, superiority, and power.

Suspicion is a dominant feature of inmate life. Prisoners are inclined to misinterpret situations, mainly because they are looking for ulterior motives in the actions of other people. Suspicion not only damages relationships but also it robs offenders of meaningful opportunities for personal development. Inmates have difficulty trusting each other on any level. They know how far they will go to survive in their environment; therefore, they also know the manipulative capacity of their peers.

Prison relationships are tense, complex, and always changing. Crowded conditions, diversity, and personal struggles all combine to create a community where feelings are unstable. Paranoia is inevitable, and manipulation is a natural survival mechanism. For some residents, survival means withdrawing from the population altogether, while for others it means identifying with those who have power. But no matter what type of friendships a prisoner develops, they all revolve around survival. Inmates do what they perceive is necessary to protect themselves.

Correctional facilities challenge the will and fortitude of every resident, and those who appear weak become victims of abuse. Aggressive inmates constantly seek out individuals to intimidate. Sexual favors, extortion, gifts, and various acts of labor are just a few of the demands placed on victims. Although some felons act alone in these endeavors, others intimidate in groups. Their collective power must be taken seriously, because there is always someone in the group who will follow through with threats.

Jealousies are another aspect of inmate relationships, and they can translate into resentment, threats, false accusations, and assaults. In these small societies of damaged egos, anyone receiving recognition is susceptible to unfavorable responses from peers, and jealousy is one of them. Jealousies are found in every area of inmate life. Inmates can become jealous of privileges and positions, legal gains, financial success, possessions, relationships, shorter prison sentences, special talents, and prison releases. Jealousy is sometimes so strong that inmates who are completing their imprisonment resist sharing their joy with peers. Because they fear resentful acts, these inmates also hesitate to leave personal items with friends who are still incarcerated.

In their jealousy, some prisoners falsely accuse other residents of improper behavior in order to promote suspicion and discord. Occasionally, convicted criminals exert tremendous energy to prove their superiority, and they are defensive of any categorization or comparison to other prisoners. Some inmates even fabricate stories about their peers to prove that they are better than them.

Every type of crime occurs in prison, from petty thefts to homicide. Thefts and assaults are common incidents, and so prisoners must exercise extreme caution. Inmates who are in debt to other prisoners for narcotics, gambling, or store items find themselves in a precarious situation if they are late with their payments. All threats should be taken seriously because some prisoners are quite capable of violence.

Almost anything can produce the spark that ignites assaults and major disturbances. Although many attacks are made beyond the view of others, such is not always the case. In fact, tensions tend to heighten when large numbers of residents congregate in one place—for example, exercise yards and cafeterias. Security officers must use extreme caution when disturbances occur in these areas.

In one instance, an assault took place during a Sunday morning worship service at Rockview. I was serving Holy Communion and enjoying the bonding effects of the Spirit, the choir was singing, and we were all caught up in God's forgiving presence. But this beautiful spirit was soon to be broken. Immediately after the service I learned that while we were receiving the Eucharist, an inmate was stabbed to death in the exercise yard adjacent to the chapel. For a brief hour our souls were raptured from the tensions of our environment, only to be thrust back to the realities of prison life. Staff people tend to forget the danger of working in a prison, but these situations quickly bring things back into focus.

In terms of property damage and injury, the 1989 riot at the State Correctional Institution at Camp Hill was Pennsylvania's worst prison disturbance. The continuing effects from this violence are beyond comprehension. Some Camp Hill inmates who were eventually transferred to Rockview experienced emotional problems and fears that previously did not exist. One inmate told me that since the riot he is nervous and easily frightened over insignificant matters. Other offenders experienced flashbacks, loss of sleep, and mistrust of the penal system.

The possibility of a riot looms over every prisoner, and this situation in itself brings stress. The majority of inmates are vehemently opposed to any manner of violence, realizing that disturbances benefit no one. Not only do they fear personal injury and the destruction of their own property but also they dread the administrative response to violence, which is usually loss of privileges. Most felons want to serve their sentence quietly, taking advantage of programs and activities that will facilitate parole. But influences, threats, and circumstances can draw the unwilling into peer turmoil.

Yet, even in all the relational strife, prisoners can form supportive and nurturing friendships. Many offenders only have each other because they have lost contact with loved ones outside the prison. If they are forced to terminate these friendships they may become severely depressed. Friendships can be broken up when felons are moved, either within the institution or to another facility. Similarly, a friend's release from the prison system is very traumatic for the inmate who is still incarcerated. Paradoxically, the struggle inherent in all inmate relationships is that while they search for intimacy, their environment makes it largely impossible.

Inmate Diversity

Prisons contain men and women from various cultural, racial, religious, and socioeconomic backgrounds. These distinctions reflect different belief systems and responses. A prisoner's self-perception is understood in the context of his or her background and family influences. Prisoners normally provide support for those who share similar backgrounds, but diversity is sometimes used as a weapon of prejudice against others.

Inmate diversity is evident in religious beliefs. Religion is a popular subject in prison, even for inmates who claim to be atheists. Inmates have extensive discussions over interpretations of religious laws and areas of personal conscience. Individuals of all faiths desire a religious code with well-defined rules and commands. Even spiritually objective prisoners gravitate toward a legalistic form of righteousness. For inmates, trying to live a "life of grace" is too abstract and uncertain, whereas "religious law" provides a concrete structure. Rigidity brings a sense of security to apprehensive people because they know what is right and what is wrong. Rules also provide simple solutions to complex issues, seemingly eliminating the struggle and testing that accompanies spiritual formation.

Many offenders pride themselves in their religious accomplishments, making certain that peers and staff know about their achievements. These same people are inclined to become self-appointed religious experts and judges of human behavior. This is common in the church, but in prison congregations it is exaggerated. As in other penal situations, the need for recognition and power has a direct relationship to religion. During my ministry at Rockview I have repeatedly been approached by residents who claim to have some special gift that elevates them above the crowd.

Unrealistic Expectations

It is common for offenders to experience stress as a result of unrealistic expectations in their relationships, education, employment, court cases, or a combination of anticipated future events. Rather than being realistic and working toward obtainable goals, these prisoners engage in escapism and fantasy. This response is destructive because it lays the groundwork for failure and disappointment.

Fantasy helps prisoners deal with their predicament, but it also blocks personal development, which is evident when a prisoner returns to society. I have listened to numerous inmates talk about their future plans; regretfully, much of what I have heard has been manufactured to make the prisoner feel good. Such visions, however, quickly vanish when the indigent offender leaves prison without marketable skills. Needless to say, the likelihood of these men and women returning to prison is very high.

Persons who do not fulfill their dreams frequently blame others. Some inmates refuse to acknowledge their mistakes or take responsibility for their lives. Instead, it is easier for them to become victims who use aggression and crime to improve their situation.

Without honest self-examination inmates cannot resolve pertinent life issues. But confronting problems is difficult for prisoners, mainly because of the pain they have already experienced through incarceration. They want to believe that their situation will somehow change with the passing of time, and escapism is simply their way of trying to eliminate what they refuse to confront.

Interactions with Staff

The incarcerated live a dehumanizing existence that is sometimes reinforced by prison employees. Inmate categorization and the reduction of people to institutional numbers demoralize prisoners, but the apathy and antagonism of prison staff is an even bigger problem. Employees often use obscenity, verbal degradation, and racism—all of which are forms of psychological violence that can easily incite individuals to aggressive acts, including prison riots.

Prison staff are under severe environmental stress and, for security and safety reasons, they must function within strict guidelines. Yet, they should be sensitive to inmate needs and requests, keeping in mind the emotional state of imprisoned people. Felons appreciate the smallest responses, and although they may not expect to receive answers to their questions, they do respect staff members who listen to them. With few exceptions, even the most difficult prisoners appreciate the responses of courteous employees. Inmates are very perceptive, and they are aware of institutional restrictions and employee stress. Therefore, many of their complaints can be resolved by a sympathetic listener who makes an effort to help. Usually, staff members only need to provide an inmate with suggestions or alternative solutions to a problem.

Prisoners often come to staff already knowing that there is no solution to their problem. In these cases, the reason they approach an employee is merely to be heard. This avenue may be the only outlet available to them. Correctional employees could do a great service if they understood this need and responded accordingly. Staff members can be very influential in an offender's life. In many instances, employees provide the encouragement and example that can change a prisoner. Institutional employees are an inmate's only role models other than his or her peers.

Regardless of position, though, all employees must share the goal to offer encouragement and promote self-worth. Most felons desire to change, but in the tense and apathetic environment of prison it can be a struggle. When we assess an inmate's collective stress, the difficulty with rehabilitation is understandable. Add the apathy and antagonism of employees to an inmate's already-existing stress, and the problem is magnified. Forming positive relationships with prisoners requires sensitivity, tolerance, and patience. Prison staff must focus on human need, rather than an inmate's crimes and imperfections. Granted, these are not easy disciplines to conquer, but they are essential elements of correctional work. Staff members have everything to gain by treating inmates with respect. Yet, few institutions emphasize empathy.

Residents continuously receive conflicting or false messages from employees, often the result of the stress and limitations placed on staff. Numerous inmate needs, extensive administrative duties, and inflexible regulations all create immense stress for prison workers. These tensions increase when employees are also dealing with personal troubles. Transference and countertransference continuously occur between inmates and employees.

Management staff are confronted by residents who anticipate immediate solutions to complicated issues. The inability to adequately respond to these requests creates stress at both ends. In some instances staff members avoid inmates who are looking for answers. While this response may help alleviate the employee's immediate stress, it ultimately increases inmate tensions. Often, employees hesitate to make certain decisions, primarily because of the damage that can result from poor judgment and mistakes. In their anxiety, staff members sometimes deny or retract promises that were made to inmates. This behavior leads supervisory personnel to be noncommittal or to pass responsibility onto others.

Inmate Visits
Family members and friends who maintain contact through personal visits provide the most support for the incarcerated, but few prisoners receive regular visits because of problems related to distance, transportation, finances, and relational tensions. Many felons are housed at institutions that are far from their family and friends. These arrangements damage mutual support systems and the prisoner's ability to nurture relationships during the separation, which adversely affects progress and rehabilitation in prison.

Although visits are important, they can create stress for both visitors and residents. Many feelings surface in inmates and their loved ones—joy and laughter, as well as sadness and tears. Displays of anger are infrequent, but at times someone can lose control. It is agonizing for families and friends to sit in supervised visiting rooms with the people they love, particularly when the inmate's children are present. During these visits each person experiences his or her own pain, and at the same time grieves for the others who are present. I have known felons who actually removed an individual's name from their visiting list because it was too painful to see that person.

Incoming Mail
To guard against contraband entering institutions, incoming mail is opened by designated staff members. Although a necessary chore, residents become suspicious when they do not receive mail that was allegedly sent to them. They sometimes believe that their incoming mail is being tampered with or, in some instances, prevented from being delivered. While probably not true, unexplained occurrences of lost mail increase the inmate's mistrust.

Incoming mail is a prisoner's lifeline to the outside world—a channel for both present and future support. Letters and packages help fill the void in offenders' lives, especially when their loved ones cannot contact them through visits and telephone calls. Incoming mail reestablishes a prisoner's roots, brings pleasurable thoughts, and provides a sense of security and belonging. In some cases, incoming mail is the primary motivator for an offender's self-improvement.

Although some of the packaged items are not essential, other packages contain items that prisoners need but cannot afford to purchase, such as winter clothing and undergarments. But to prisoners, any gift mailed from the outside is highly valued and protected, particularly if it is sent by family members.

Packages that enter institutions come under strict regulations, and certain items are prohibited. The rules for receiving these packages can be frustrating for both sender and receiver. If mailings do not explicity adhere to institutional guidelines, they are returned. While prison officials have legitimate safety concerns with incoming packages, they need to reevaluate mailing procedures that have nothing to do with threats to security and safety. For example, prisoners are not allowed to receive articles of clothing that have certain manufactured logos on them. Prisons have a tendency to retain archaic rules that do nothing more than frustrate people. Moreover, some administrators fear modifying or removing policies that are no longer pertinent.

Outgoing Correspondence

Except for restrictions that prohibit inmates from communicating between prisons, penal residents can write to whomever they please. The struggle for inmates is finding positive things to write about. This situation is also true for the recipients of inmate mail, many of whom are working through changes and feelings resulting from the incarceration. Letter writing, although it is important, commonly becomes sparse because of the pain involved in communication.

Another problem develops when felons lack the basic writing skills they need to maintain contact. Those with limited abilities undergo a humiliation and discouragement that often curtails their written communications. Family and friends may interpret this lack of communication as intentional neglect, which can create relational strife.

Still another issue involves inmates writing to their children. A number of convicted criminals have children out of wedlock, frequently from more than one relationship. Many of these children have had little or no contact with the incarcerated parent. When offenders try to reestablish ties with their children they send letters to the last known address. But these earnest attempts are often futile because the other parent has moved or refuses to respond. Moreover, their children may react with confusion and anger. While offenders must blame themselves for most of these hardships, it is a sad plight for those who have truly changed their ways.

Telephone Communications

Inmates can only make outgoing telephone calls by using public systems and reversing the charges. They must also attain approved scheduling with a block sergeant or other supervisor. Although the cost of the call places a financial burden on other people, some prisoners are persistent in making collect calls to family members and friends. However, when the telephone bills exceed a certain amount telephone companies can place electronic blocks on the services of those who are being called, sometimes at the customer's request. Some prisoners become quite agitated when they learn of these blocks. Rather than being understanding, they interpret it as a personal affront.

Other than emergency calls placed through a staff member, usually made in the office of a chaplain or counselor, inmates must use the public telephones in the cell blocks. Often such calls are made from an overcrowded and noisy environment, and if the prisoner does not make contact, the scheduling and authorization process must be repeated. Incoming calls for residents can only be received by certain staff members, and they must be of an emergency nature.

The tensions resulting from restricted telephone use lead many prisoners to forego such efforts. Scheduling problems, inability to reach people, environmental irritations, and need to reverse the charges all translate into excessive inmate stress. Often, inmate confrontations will occur over telephone usage.

Tensions also develop from counterproductive telephone conversations. It is not unusual for inmate calls to progress into hostile arguments. Rather than relieving stress, most telephone conversations persistently aggravate it, much of it the result of unresolved issues within the family circle.

Heterosexual Intimacy

Only inmates assigned to community programs and those with furlough status have opportunities for heterosexual intimacy. This deprivation produces both conscious and unconscious stress—most people would agree that relational intimacy promotes emotional health. Because it is related to one's sense of belonging, the absence of intimacy can produce feelings of isolation, insecurity, and incompleteness. Individuals who live without intimacy may eventually begin to experience doubts about their sexual abilities.

Inmates nearing their release date experience anxiety concerning sex. The machismo role that prisoners play hides a multitude of insecurities, including those of a sexual nature. The length of a person's prison sentence is significant—in working with male inmates, for example, I have seen a correlation between sexual insecurities and long incarcerations.

Imprisonment also causes some offenders who were not previously gay to engage in homosexual activities. This behavior may be a result of sexual insecurity; it may also be a way to relieve sexual frustration, stop threats, or promote personal gain. Although the reasons for homosexual activities vary, there is little doubt that such involvements increase an inmate's emotional turmoil, creating new areas of guilt, jealousies, and rivalries. Moreover, these prisoners risk the transfer and spread of disease.

New inmates, especially the young, can find themselves confronted by individuals who engage in homosexual behavior. When new prisoners resist homosexual advances they are plagued by threats and various forms of harassment. These threats may eventually lead to assault or rape. I have known inmates who chose solitary confinement to avoid this torment.

Inmate Weddings

Some inmates actively seek marriage partners. Couples who have prison weddings often knew each other prior to the incarceration, possibly parenting one or more children. Nevertheless, some relationships have been initiated and developed during the imprisonment. These friendships normally begin through letter writing and progress to prison visits. But regardless of how the relationships commence, most of them involve enormous mutual need. Offenders not only have deep emotional needs but also they have financial and legal ones. Parole approval requires employment and housing, and a new spouse can help meet these demands.

Prison marriages are based on unrealistic expectations and little interpersonal knowledge. The continued separation of the couple tends to increase tension and create new demands. This tension, combined with unmet needs and an increasing knowledge of spousal imperfections, often results in troubled relationships and, ultimately, divorce.

Chaplains are responsible for pre-marriage interviews. These dialogues are intended to stimulate the couple to reflect on important relational issues, allowing them time to resolve personal differences before they are married. In the interview, couples should discuss the specific trials that face inmate marriages. In addition, prison clergy should examine the level of honesty between the two individuals.

My experiences with inmate marriage interviews have not been positive. In fact, I have seen very few of these relationships exhibit any foundational strengths. In the majority of cases both parties were very immature, lacking forethought and comprehension of basic marital issues. Also, their individual needs prevented mutual support and nurturing. Few marriages can survive this negativity. However, in spite of the warning signs, most couples believe that their nuptials will somehow overshadow the problems. These marriages generally result in a brief and devastating union.

Life-Cycle Transitions

Life changes are extremely difficult in prison, essentially because encouragement and support systems are inadequate. While inmates can sympathize with their peers, they are often too consumed by their own problems to be helpful. Because prisoners are preoccupied with themselves, they are not sensitive to the needs of their fellow residents. Without the concern and support of others, the incarcerated go through trials and life changes alone. Moreover, prisons seldom offer programs that focus on the needs of particular age groups.

Young offenders realize that some of their best years are vanishing. The excitement of youth is replaced with a world where joy is found in fleeting moments, rather than extended experiences. But in a prison community where power rules, young inmates assume much of the control. This power and control gives them purpose. There are always older residents who still have power, but they are few in number.

As inmates get older they see the futility and danger in aggression, and they begin to withdraw from role play and power struggles. This is also true of people in free society, because aging not only slows us down but hopefully instills wisdom. Older prisoners are retrospective and more concerned about relationships than power. They have a heightened sense of mortality because they realize that they have little time left.

Older inmates often feel isolation and despair as their lives near conclusion without relational intimacy, family fulfillment, and meaningful accomplishments. Lost opportunities accompany wrong decisions and regret for acts committed years ago. Young prisoners may still have visions of the future, but aging felons become fatalistic and alienated as their dreams and goals dissipate. The predominance of youth among the prison population only adds to feelings of loneliness in older prisoners. They fear that they will become terminally ill and die alone in prison.

Aging, in varying degrees, affects the transitional periods and personal development of all inmates. The fear of aging in prison, although more prevalent within particular age groups, is found in every prisoner. Human needs are constantly in flux, and inmates are no exception. Yet, prisoners live in an environment void of the resources that carry other people through crises. Whether they are entering adulthood, middle age, or the senior years, prisoners receive little understanding and compassion from peers and staff. Life changes are difficult enough when individuals have support from others and a healthy self-concept, but offenders are deficient in both of these areas.

Legal Process

Inmates direct their anger toward the legal system as a whole, but the majority of their complaints are against defense lawyers—both public defenders and private attorneys. Many inmates have shared their court experiences with me, and with few exceptions their complaints are the same. While some people are quick to believe that all convicted criminals are dissatisfied with their defense, it does not negate the prisoners' allegations. The observations I made during my police career parallel inmate claims.

Prisoners assert that defense lawyers give shallow and misleading explanations, fail to respond to telephone calls and written correspondence, spend inadequate time in case preparation, and charge excessive fees. These fees are often paid by family members who must borrow money, sell possessions, or mortgage and even sell their homes. Criminal attorneys know that desperate people will somehow obtain legal fees.

Using a public defender may eliminate financial concerns, but other problems still exist. These lawyers carry large caseloads and have little time for court preparation. Many defendants do not see their public defender until the week of trial, which undoubtedly impairs their defense. When we consider the magnitude of some cases and the potential prison sentence involved, such behavior indicates that the legal system has major flaws.

A large number of public defenders are inexperienced in criminal cases. In fact, some of them are recent law school graduates. These individuals acquire their positions to gain knowledge of the legal system and make professional contacts. While this may benefit the attorney, it can spell disaster for the defendant. Moreover, public defenders and district attorneys sometimes make agreements to ease the burden of going to trial at the expense of the defendant.

When the defendant is incarcerated, new difficulties surface. Prisoners become frustrated as they proceed with legal appeals and other lawsuits. Their lack of expertise and finances places them in a hopeless situation. Often they use the legal services of a knowledgeable peer, which can be more effective than trying to communicate with attorneys and various agencies.

The appeal process keeps hope alive for prisoners, but legal rejections quickly diminish that hope. They cling to the smallest chance for freedom or a reduced prison sentence, and when legal avenues prove unsuccessful, they must work through their frustrations. This is a crucial time for inmates, particularly if they have a long minimum sentence. Up to now they have survived their environment with the hope of positive court action. Some offenders live off this hope for years, and it is never realized.

While the majority of these prisoners eventually find ways to adjust, some of them develop chronic depression. I have counseled a number of inmates whose court appeals were denied, some of whom appeared emotionally unable to serve their sentence. Fortunately, even these individuals seem to find the strength and the resources to continue.

Not all felons who receive legal rejections become depressed. Career criminals, for example, are continuously involved in legal pursuits, although they are seldom optimistic about the outcome. Their legal research meets other needs, such as the desire for knowledge and recognition. This work occupies time and helps build self-esteem.

The parole process is another legal concern. Prisoners who are going through parole procedures lack assistance, including sufficient access to parole representatives, counselors, and other staff members who can be helpful. Successful parole requires both inside networking and contact with outside sources, which is not possible without institutional assistance. The indifference of staff members may actually prevent someone from obtaining parole, which can result in unnecessary suffering for inmates and their families.

There is nothing more important to prisoners than parole; it consumes their thoughts and energy. However, institutional contradictions, changes in counselors, and insufficient interest bring confusion and stress. A prisoner may not be certain of parole requirements because too many voices of authority send mixed messages. A counselor may be the primary decision maker, but the influence of psychologists, block managers, security staff, and other administrators can change the rules. A counselor may direct an inmate toward a specific treatment plan only to have it altered by other staff members. When changes take place near the end of an offender's minimum sentence, it can mean continued imprisonment.

Personnel changes can also affect parole. Correctional staff frequently change their status through promotion, in-house reorganization, or transfer. This change in status affects inmates who are under their supervision. Residents need counselors and other staff who are cognizant of their advancements, which is difficult when personnel are constantly changing. Losing a counselor with whom prisoners have developed a rapport can also be a significant setback in attaining parole.

Institutional Rejections

Prisoners live with rejection. They are continuously seeking ways to increase self-esteem and recognition—necessary ingredients for their survival in such a harsh environment. The principal method of achieving self-worth in prison is to take advantage of educational and training programs. While various inmates waste their time, others are motivated to accomplish all they can during their incarceration. Some offenders even participate in demanding programs, such as completing high school or college equivalency tests.

In correctional facilities where worthwhile programs do exist, there is a great demand to participate—but space limitations restrict involvement. This situation creates intense peer competition and jealousy. Some individuals are placed on waiting lists, but others are turned away because they fail to meet education and security requirements.

Regardless of the reason they are turned away, prisoners who are not allowed to participate in a desired program feel the increasing weight of rejection. Some felons view these programs as their last chance for self-improvement. Rather than considering the institution's reason for refusing them, they tend to take the rejection personally and see it as another example of failure.

Rejection is also experienced by those who are accepted into programs but are unable to grasp the work. These failures can become prophetic, causing individuals to resist future involvement in programs. To complicate matters, the inactivity resulting from their disengagement intensifies their stress.

Although rejection is an unavoidable aspect of life, particular circumstances can make any negative response devastating to some people. The instability and low self-esteem of prisoners puts them in this category, and staff members must be careful not to undermine an offender's trauma.

Medical Care

When inmates become ill, life in prison is even more difficult. The prison setting is simply not conducive to the healing process. The suspicion and mistrust that pervades penal institutions affects inmate health care. Prisoners view health employees as part of an oppressive and apathetic system. They feel that their criminal status interferes with their treatment and claim that medical staff antagonize them with various forms of psychological punishment.

Prisons normally employ a sufficient number of medical professionals, but often their attitudes can be a problem. In the high-intensity work of prison health care, the perspective and mission of these employees easily can become distorted. The demands and manipulation of some inmates only add to their stress. Anxiety and discord related to medical care is a serious problem in our prisons, especially with the increasing number of seriously ill residents that results from overcrowding.

Chaplains hear numerous complaints from prisoners about medical treatment. Many of their grievances are either exaggerated or unfounded, but enough of them are substantiated to justify concern. Inmates who request medical attention for common ailments normally receive adequate care, but often those with difficult or chronic cases do not. Medical staff are inclined to disregard complaints of pain, often delaying complete physical examinations and hospital tests. Inmates must also deal with long treatment lines, an inability to consult with physicians, inadequate physical rehabilitation, and difficulty obtaining follow-up care and second opinions. Prisoners who need continuing treatment must face these problems everyday.

Inmates understandably fear for their health when they are recuperating from an illness or surgery. Most surgical procedures are performed in community hospitals, but prisoners are returned to correctional facilities upon discharge. After an observation period in the prison dispensary, they return to their cell block. Prisoners must heal from illness and surgery in these harsh conditions.

Another problem is the availability of expedient assistance should an inmate need medical help. For example, housing units average one officer for every sixty to one hundred inmates. This means that a cell block of five hundred prisoners has only six or seven officers on duty at a given time. A long period could pass before security staff became aware of a medical emergency. Large cell blocks that have two or more tiers present additional problems, particularly if the emergency occurs at the far end of an upper level.

Inmates become soulful when their peers have medical problems, realizing that the same thing could happen to them. But their ultimate fear is that they will suffer a terminal disease without the compassionate presence of family and friends and die in a prison infirmary or hospital far from home.

My visits with terminally ill prisoners have been painful. Their loneliness and despair cannot be compared to anything I have encountered in my ministry. Seeing the faces of inmates dying of AIDS or cancer renders one speechless. What can be said to comfort an inmate who is dying alone in a state prison? In my experience, all we can do is pray for the grace that is offered during these times. Prison ministry has taught me not to struggle for the proper words. Instead, a prayerful and compassionate presence is important to a suffering person.

The same diseases that claim members of society obviously affect prisoners as well. The difference is in the availability of compassion, comfort, and support systems; the amount of environmental stress; and the quality of medical care. When these elements are lacking, the suffering is increased. Circumstances often improve when dying felons are moved to community hospitals. After an inmate's death, the other residents are left to ponder a fate that could be their own. They reflect on the uncertainties of life and the depth of human pain.

Economic Loss

Incarceration places acute restrictions on financial income and purchasing power. Employment in many prisons is sparse, and some
facilities provide no job opportunities, particularly local and county
prisons. But even in larger institutions where inmates can obtain
employment, they earn as little as seventeen cents an hour. This
money is normally used for toiletries, cigarettes, and food snacks.
Residents who desire other items must depend on their family and
friends. Although prisoners are supplied with their basic needs, the
loss of income also prevents them from preparing for their eventual
release. Even when employment is available, small incomes and peer
conflicts tend to destroy the incentive to work. Prisoners may become
jealous of certain positions and use peer pressure to steal articles
from work sites.

Imprisonment creates other areas of economic stress. For example, inmates usually lose their major possessions, such as their cars or
their homes, because they are unable to make the required payments. This situation also creates credit problems for offenders and
their immediate families. Prisoners experience additional financial
stress if they file legal appeals. Private attorneys require substantial
retainers to continue a court case.

Financial troubles account for a considerable amount of peer con-
tention. In an attempt to gain power, some convicted criminals engage
in illicit activities, such as extortion, gambling, and the sale of contraband or commissary items. Because inmates are not permitted to possess currency, they pay their debts with cigarette packs or twice the
amount of the item they received. Prisoners who sell contraband set a
time limit for the payment, and the limit is strictly enforced. Late or
unpaid debts may lead to increased payments, threats, or assaults.

Inmates are subject to threats and assaults even for very small
amounts. Taking advantage of someone who is operating an illegal
store is viewed as a direct attack against established power, which is
not tolerated. Being lenient with a debtor would be considered weak
and communicate a false message to other patrons and prospective
borrowers. Felons engage in illegal sales to make money and establish power and control; therefore, challenges to their authority are
met with convincing force. Many brutal assaults occur over debts of
less than ten dollars. Yet, even a few dollars is wealth to people who
have nothing.

Some residents use their creative ingenuity to earn money by making greeting cards, crafts, and different types of artwork. Many of the prisoners who purchase these items send them to family members and friends. Every institution has residents with artistic talent, and their abilities are in demand. But some offenders threaten these individuals in order to obtain free work, causing talented inmates to refrain from advertising their skills.

Economic stress is most conspicuous when felons return to society. Leaving prison untrained and indigent places them in a vulnerable position. The transition from prison to society is overwhelming enough, but an individual's inability to gain employment can drive him or her back to criminal activity. While prison was certainly a hardship, it did satisfy basic needs that are costly in society, such as food, housing, and clothing. The high cost of living is often forgotten by the incarcerated.

Those leaving prison find that the economy has changed significantly. The longer their prison sentence, the harder it is for them to adjust to this change. The move from a community where purchases consisted of toilet articles and food snacks to a society in which even working people live in poverty can be quite a shock. In their attempt to survive, some released felons revert back to a life of crime. Even criminals who desire to change may find their new lives too strenuous. On the other hand, some discharged felons never really left their life of crime.

Influences from Other Institutions

Disturbances at one penal institution can affect population moods at other facilities. Prisoners quickly become aware of perceived injustices within the correctional system. These instances promote a type of peer empathy that encompasses anger toward prison administrators. Such tensions are capable of sparking aggressive behavior.

During the riot at Pennsylvania's Camp Hill facility, for example, some prisoners at Rockview openly voiced their support for the inmate violence. These individuals wanted staff members to know that the same action was possible at our institution. In varying degrees, this subtle intimidation lasted for several weeks. Although these threats were mostly ways of ventilating frustration and anger, they could have provoked a disturbance. The truth, however, is that most inmates do not advocate violence to make a statement.

Regardless of distance, a bond does exist between the incarcerated. Convicted felons consider themselves oppressed by the system as a whole; therefore, they identify with all penal injustice. Events that transpire at other prisons are often taken personally by inmates. Those who actively seek institutional changes follow events at other prisons very carefully, especially the outcome of grievances and lawsuits. Prisoners view legal cases won by other inmates as collective victories.

Educational Deficiencies

A large percentage of criminals do not have a high school education, and very few have been exposed to cultural and religious diversity. This affects inmate relationships and personal growth. Prisoners develop personalities that lack sensitivity, tolerance, and acceptance. They view differences with suspicion, and resist rational thinking.

Prisoners with educational limitations have fewer outlets for ventilation, which causes tensions to build. Inability to participate in the constructive activities that education makes possible leads these inmates to a destructive idleness. While many prisons offer basic skills classes, insecurities and embarrassment prevent some residents from attending them. The pressure to appear tough is another reason inmates do not participate in these programs. Admitting to a weakness contradicts an image of power and control.

Nevertheless, institutions with extensive educational programs find that inmates are very interested in their classes. Teachers are amazed at the advances made by prisoners. Whether they are enrolled in basic skills classes or college-level courses, learning enhances their self-esteem and motivates them to continue their education. Personal development decreases tensions, creating positive attitudes and objectivity. People who feel good about themselves develop better relationships, which can be seen in prisoners who participate in educational programs. These inmates also serve as an example to their peers.

Nothing is more exciting for inmates than concrete accomplishments. For many prisoners, prison educational programs are the first opportunity they have had for serious learning beyond high school, and the personal rewards are many. Education gives them a new outlook on a life that is filled with possibilities. Some residents become so excited about their educational accomplishments that they investigate opportunities for education at universities and trade schools beyond the prison walls.

Ignorance and idleness destroy incentive and damage relationships. When members of society reject the idea of inmate education, they fail to comprehend the results of their reasoning. This kind of revenge against convicted offenders only aggravates an increasing crime rate.

Unresolved Anger

The undercurrent of inmate anger is a potentially explosive reality in prisons. Inmates do not fully comprehend the reasons for their anger, and prison employees are not adequately trained to respond. Prisons are full of people who are living on the edge of an emotional cliff, and their rage is easily ignited. As such, prison employees must be sensitive to inmate needs and respond accordingly. I myself have watched inmate moods change rapidly from one extreme to another in a matter of seconds. A prisoner's calm can suddenly turn to rage and then, almost immediately, back to calm again. Staff who do not understand the reasons for these sudden vacillations may respond inappropriately.

Most inmates readily admit to strong inner conflicts, often targeting individuals or circumstances that they believe contribute to or cause their problems. Yet, it is difficult for them to move beyond this point to a broader understanding of the events that caused their anger. Like most people, the incarcerated simply feel pain and react spontaneously to alleviate it. But unlike those in society, inmates have few resources to help them work through their many feelings.

A certain amount of displaced anger is common to everyone; hence, it is accepted without much thought. Those who briefly lose their temper in a stable environment are seldom a threat to order and human life. But anger in the prison setting is quite different, mainly because it is more intense, widespread, and concentrated in a dehumanizing atmosphere where negativity prevails.

Large populations, staff shortages, and insufficiently trained employees make it impossible for penal institutions to address the problem of inmate anger. Inmates are placed in psychological categories, and any chance of therapeutic help is consumed by an impersonal and overburdened system. Without radical changes in corrections philosophy, these conditions will persist. Inmates need a safe, therapeutic place to ventilate their frustrations.

Inmate insolence and aggression are clear messages that their anger is real and that officials must listen for the causes to avoid disturbances.

Prison riots are the result of collective anger, and they have many lingering effects. Not only are inmates and staff traumatized, but their families become victims as well. In addition, communities develop mistrust toward a system that is responsible for their safety. Few citizens want a prison in their backyard, and when major disturbances occur, their anxieties are reinforced.

When we consider the degree of anger in our prisons, it is surprising that there is not more violence. I am always amazed at the discipline in prison communities. The reason for this order, however, does not require extensive analysis, nor can it be attributed to governmental expertise. Most inmates work very hard to maintain positive behavior. They know what is expected of them—specifically, what actions will facilitate their parole—and they try to keep within the acceptable limits.

Negative behavior from inmates strains relationships with staff, especially counselors who are authorized to initiate parole. The release of anger, even if it is brief and unintentional, can bring severe punishment to prisoners, such as the termination of employment programs and furloughs. Solitary confinement and parole setbacks are other possible results of unrestrained anger. Needless to say, these are strong incentives for exercising self-control.

Some inmates utilize valuable programs, making remarkable strides toward rehabilitation and future success. I have known offenders who received both their high school diploma and college degree while they were imprisoned. Although great achievements for a prisoner, they have little influence on staff and parole boards if the inmate continues to exhibit a poor attitude. Some felons have repeatedly surmounted obstacles only to experience failure because of combative behavior.

A large percentage of felons come from fragmented families, and many of them did not receive encouragement and support from their families during childhood. This does not mean that they were not loved but that the love was not communicated in concrete and understandable ways.

Encouragement and support from parents promotes feelings of self-worth and hope, as well as a sense of belonging and security. Inmate anger can often be traced back to a lack of parental encouragement. Emotional support in a person's developmental years helps alleviate the confusion, fears, guilt, and ambivalent feelings that give birth to anger. Also, families that fail to express love and encouragement often have children who cannot express these feelings either, which becomes evident in their belief systems, attitudes, and relationships.

Inmates who attempt to work through their anger find it very difficult. Enduring institutional stress, lack of therapeutic assistance, and continuing personal afflictions combine to produce a mood that resists treatment. In addition, the incarcerated are preoccupied with the need to develop coping mechanisms and make the adjustments necessary for survival. These matters consume an inmate's energy and time, taking precedence over less important concerns, such as education and spiritual growth. Their goal is to get through each day; therefore, they give little thought to therapeutic processes. When a chaplain asks prisoners how things are going, their common response is, "One day at a time." This brief expression reveals inmate priorities.

Anger is often difficult to detect because inmates sometimes direct their rage inward. Role play and denial may hide these emotions from others, but they still exist. Offenders remain angry at themselves for committing the crimes that caused their imprisonment. They also regret having damaged relationships with others, primarily family members. These impaired relationships are a continual source of guilt and pain for convicted criminals. Prison makes a person conscious of priorities and what is important in life. Being separated from friends and family members and knowing that this separation was self-produced causes ongoing anguish. Offenders often share their feelings of regret and self-directed anger with chaplains. Contrary to society's image of convicted criminals, a large number of them manifest remorse and a desire to change.

Another reason for inmate anger is lost opportunities. Inmates recognize that they need the skills they previously rejected, and they must live with this mistake. Whether they require academic or specific occupational training, prisoners must acquire a marketable education in order to combat old patterns. Some felons look to prison educational programs for answers, but increasing demands and existing limitations close many doors.

Everyone is familiar with lost opportunities, but over time most people engage in new activities and develop other goals. Although their expectations may not have been realized, life continues to have purpose and direction. However, inmates are in a different situation, principally because their wrong decisions involved criminal

activity. Their mistakes removed them from society, and imprisonment blocks the new beginning that is possible with members of a
free community.

Offenders with drug and alcohol addictions also direct their anger
inward. The false promises and controlling forces of addiction destroy
an individual's relationships and potential. While some penal facilities have drug and alcohol programs, they seldom have the professional resources to help individuals heal. As a result, unresolved
addiction problems often bring parolees back to prison.

Capital Punishment

The State Correctional Institution at Rockview is Pennsylvania's offi-
cial site for the administration of the death penalty, which was rein-
stated in Pennsylvania in 1978. The first electrocution in Pennsylvania
took place on February 23, 1915. However, in 1991 the method of
execution was changed from electrocution to lethal injection. To
date, the state has executed three hundred and fifty people.

During my prison ministry a number of death warrants were
signed by the governor's office. For this reason, designated staff had
to be briefed on execution procedures and participate in mock drills.
My first briefings took place when the electric chair was still being
used, and the entire exercise was ghastly. The transition to lethal
injection may have eliminated some of the visual horror, but the
methodical killing of a human being remains an atrocious act.

Almost all the inmates scheduled to die at Rockview were given a
stay of execution at least one week before the appointed time. The
one exception was an individual who came within twenty-eight hours
of death. This situation allowed me to examine the mood of a prison
when an execution was about to take place.

The inmates at Rockview knew about the execution for at least
two weeks in advance, but there was little conversation about it.
Then, within forty-eight hours of the specified time, prisoners began
to express their feelings to me. They seemed to be pondering the
impending death with disbelief and shock. A number of prisoners
solicited my beliefs concerning capital punishment and wanted to
know how I felt about possibly being part of the process.

The thought of our government actually killing a person was hard
for the prisoners to grasp. The taking of life did not fit into their idea
of a legal system that claims to advocate rehabilitation. In fact, some
individuals said that capital punishment lowered the state to a crimi-

nal level. Other inmates experienced chilling emotions as they contemplated their own crimes and how they could have received the death penalty.

The execution I referred to was canceled, but the late hour required extensive interaction with prisoners on this agonizing and controversial subject. In all fairness, there were residents who supported the death penalty, but they were very few. The overall response to the scheduled execution was one of shock and sorrow that our courts could justify such an act.

Transition to Society

After serving a significant portion of their prison sentence, some felons are permitted furlough status. This status enables them to make periodic community visits to prepare for their transition back to society. The number of inmates who are allowed into the community is limited, but furloughs are a feasible goal for prisoners in certain institutions.

Those with furlough status often become anxious about an upcoming trip home. They are concerned about the possibility of something going wrong on the visit, which would jeopardize future furlough opportunities. But much of their uneasiness is simply a response to their approaching independence in a world that has become foreign to them.

While these community visits are important, they are not without their problems, one of which is the pressure exerted by fellow inmates to bring contraband back to the prison. Offenders who refuse to comply with these demands may encounter relational conflict, although assaults over these matters are rare.

Prison furloughs are normally productive even though inmates are occasionally depressed when they return. In many cases, an inmate's family situation has changed significantly during his or her incarceration. These inmates find it difficult to relate to loved ones in the same ways.

Inmates nearing the end of their prison sentence usually have ambivalent feelings. Although they are joyful with anticipation at the thought of being released, inmates fear that they will not succeed or be accepted into society. They are also apprehensive of court stipulations and their ability to maintain an amicable relationship with their parole officer. Those on parole must constantly be on guard lest they violate court regulations. Depending on the strictness of their parole officer and the seriousness of their infraction, felons can receive significant setbacks. If the parolee is charged with a criminal offense, incarceration is mandatory. However, there should be some flexibility when minor parole stipulations are violated. Returning an individual to prison for a minor infraction can be counterproductive. The advancements made by the parolee and the hardships on family members should be considered by the parole officer. Sometimes everyone is better served when these infractions do not result in more prison time.

Most released offenders return to the same environment that contributed to their crimes, and the negative influences of these surroundings are normally still present. Some of their previous friends may even welcome them back into the fold. Individuals with drug and alcohol problems find these influences overpowering, especially when things are not going well with their transition to society. This pattern is quite common for a number of people who leave prison, and they must rely on their own will and fortitude.

Some inmates acquire parole plans with community centers, employment sites, and educational programs, but these places are few in number. Moreover, such facilities generally seek certain types of parolees. For example, felons who have committed sex crimes are seldom admitted. Released criminals continually struggle for acceptance and trust from others, and the nature of their crime can be a barrier.

Upon release, inmate relationships undergo stress because of the changes that are caused by incarceration. The bond that once held an inmate's relationships together may no longer exist. Released prisoners and their families are forced to develop certain levels of independence in order to adapt to their new roles. This independence is beneficial while the individual is incarcerated, but upon release they must deal with emotional distancing.

Released offenders find it necessary to continually prove their rehabilitation, knowing that imperfections are often interpreted as regression. Rather than instilling encouragement and hope, some people persistently anticipate an offender's downfall. If the released felon believes what others expect, it is easy for him or her to fail.

Incarceration diminishes working skills, erodes self-esteem, encourages dependency, and stifles socialization. The radical transition from an isolated and dependent life to freedom and independence is an arduous one. To survive, released felons must exercise immense strength and stability.

Other Stress Factors

Holidays can have an adverse effect on people, depending on their circumstances, but they can be especially devastating for prisoners. Being imprisoned during traditional family days is trying for inmates. As holidays approach, inmates become more and more intense, and their anxiety and depression are evident. When the actual day arrives, the mood of the prison community changes to a somber acceptance. But this acceptance represses many feelings.

Immobility and limited participation in nature also generates tension. Experiencing nature and having the freedom of mobility are unconscious stress-relieving channels for everyone. Some prisoners, however, spend years living behind the concrete walls of prison where their travel is restricted to less than one square mile. Moreover, older maximum security prisons are surrounded by perimeter walls that block out the outside world.

I myself cannot imagine living in an isolated world of concrete and iron bars. Participating in the peace and beauty of God's creation is essential to my well-being, and the mere thought of losing this gift brings distress. Equally important is the mobility that allows me to experience life on many levels. Loss of these freedoms exceed the comprehension of the free person.

Inmates also experience stress when they see their peers leaving prison for community functions, furloughs, and parole, or when they have completed their maximum sentence. Prisoners who are serving long sentences are especially prone to this stress. Adjustment is easier if they are incarcerated with persons who share a similar situation. However, overcrowding forces many of these inmates into facilities where the average prison sentence is about five years.

Mundane routines, prison clothing, and idleness, while seemingly minor irritants, all bring discouragement and produce stress. There is no escape from the mechanical structures and mandates that comprise prison life, and with time this inflexible monotony takes its toll on inmates.

3

Ministry to the Incarcerated

Biblical Foundations for Ministry

Prison ministry shares the same objectives as the universal church: regeneration, healing, and spiritual development. Prison chaplains should show convicted felons the righteous path and offer them the support and resources they need to live a new life in Jesus Christ.

Jesus made it clear that he came for the sick, which includes even those guilty of the most heinous crimes (Mt 9:11–13; 25:34–46). In the cross we find a universal atonement that takes us into every penal institution: "[He] is the atoning sacrifice for our sins, and not for ours only but also for the sins of the whole world" (1 Jn 2:2; cf. 1 Tm 2:5–6). As the body of Christ, the mission of the church is to deliver the message of forgiveness and reconciliation to all people, regardless of their sins (Mk 1:15; Rom 3:24; 2 Cor 5:18–19). Therefore, to deny inmate populations the message of the Scriptures and the grace of the church is to deny the will of God and the sacrificial death of Christ.

Prison ministry is not simply a constitutional right of inmates, but also a command of the church. Matthew records a discourse in which Jesus places prisoners in the same category as the hungry and naked: ". . . I was naked and you gave me clothing, I was sick and you took care of me, I was in prison and you visited me" (Mt 25:36). Although they are confined, the incarcerated are members of the society for which Christ died. In fact, prisoners desperately need the compassion and transforming grace that is only found in Jesus Christ.

The following biblical foundations are universal, but prisoners find special meaning in them. These areas of Christian doctrine must be emphasized by the church when ministering to the incarcerated.

Forgiveness and Reconciliation

Incarceration is a gnawing reminder that we reap what we sow. It is a clear revelation that sinful living brings many forms of punishment, including legal retribution in this life. In prison, individuals are taught the vanity of false lifestyles, but in these confining environments there is also a message of hope. While lost opportunities and damaged relationships cannot be reversed, forgiveness and reconciliation can bring healing and a new beginning.

Spiritual transformation and personal growth can only be gained through divine forgiveness. Through Jesus Christ the mercy of God is available to everyone, even individuals who are guilty of the most offensive crimes. Many people find this hard to believe, including those who profess to be Christians, but it has been proven through the gospel of Jesus Christ and his church. In Jesus' message convicted criminals find cleansing, inner peace, and the hope of eternal life.

As God's forgiveness consumes our spirit, the weight of personal guilt and inner conflict begins to dissolve. Through this cleansing and renewal, we are able to forgive ourselves and others. Most prisoners live with a strong sense of guilt and failure, and some of them believe that their crimes are beyond forgiveness. Therefore, it is important for the church to include forgiveness in its total ministry, and communicate it as the very foundation for personal change, healing, and a new life.

Adoption

Human adoption of a child is rooted in love, and it is a responsibility that requires tremendous energy and commitment. The relationship of a loving parent to a child includes a sacrificial sharing of self to meet the child's needs and improve his or her life. Parents must provide comfort, encouragement, support, and hope on a daily basis.

Adoption is also a legal matter that makes the child an heir to the parent's estate. This dimension provides for the future and brings security and calm to the child. Even in the midst of adversity the adopted child can be assured that life is moving in a positive direction.

The Scriptures vividly describe God's relationship with humanity as that of a heavenly parent to a child. This spiritual adoption is made possible through divine grace and our faith in Jesus Christ. Moreover, it extends into the eschatological future when, as heirs, we will receive all that God has promised us: "Those who conquer will inherit these things, and I will be their God and they will be my children" (Rv 21:7).

Being children of God assures us of his sustaining presence. We receive inner peace and joy. Spiritual adoption means that our dwelling place is with the Creator. As we await the fulfillment of his promises we receive the benefits of his indwelling Spirit. The apostle Paul tells us, "[We] ourselves, who have the first fruits of the Spirit, groan inwardly while we wait for adoption, the redemption of our bodies" (Rom 8:23). In the meantime, Christ promises not to forsake us as orphans, but instead to send us the Comforter in times of trial (Jn 14:15–20).

Many prisoners feel abandoned by family members and significant others. These feelings may be exaggerated or even false, but they reveal the prisoner's emotional state. The biblical concept of adoption provides offenders with a renewed identity and sense of belonging to both God and God's family. It also helps them realize that God is a parent who, out of love, will provide for their continuing needs as he did through the death and resurrection promises of Jesus Christ.

Divine Grace and Personal Faith

God's grace can be understood as a clemency in which he gives himself to humanity. Hebrew Scripture writers reveal individuals, such as Moses, David, and Job, who both sought and received divine grace, but the apostle Paul provides theological insights into God's selflessness (Gal 1:6, 15). Paul states that we are justified freely through the atonement of Christ, and grace comes to us through faith: "For sin will have no dominion over you, since you are not under law but under grace" (Rom 6:14; cf. Gal 2:21; 5:5–6; Eph 2:8–9).

In his letter to the Corinthians, Paul wrote that it was grace that changed him: "But by the grace of God I am what I am . . ." (1 Cor 15:10). He also informed the Ephesians that grace is given to everyone in accordance with Christ's apportionment: "But each of us was given grace according to the measure of Christ's gift" (Eph 4:7). Grace makes personal growth possible because it provides a channel for the communication with the Spirit (2 Pt 3:18). There is a direct relationship between grace and the exercise of faith. The author of Hebrews wrote, "Let us therefore approach the throne of grace with boldness, so that we may receive mercy and find grace to help in time of need" (Heb 4:16).

Grace is a powerful gift for individuals who have been devastated by past sins and whose present lives are a daily struggle. Like all people, felons must understand that they are not removed from tribulation, but through grace and faith they can be sustained and even transformed to the glory of God. Paul's weakness in the midst of his trials enabled him to experience God's power, which strengthened his faith and service. Paul's experience can bring both personal and collective hope to inmate populations.

Rest and Peace

The Bible develops a theme of *rest*, which is necessary for our emotional and spiritual welfare. In the Hebrew Scriptures, rest is more of a physical need, but the spiritual implications of rest are presented by Christ in the Gospels—for example, he promises rest for the human soul: "Come to me, all you that are weary and are carrying heavy burdens, and I will give you rest" (Mt 11:28). This biblical promise also has futuristic significance. The land of Canaan was an imperfect rest that foreshadowed the eternal rest in God (Rv 14:13). God's desire for humans to be at rest reflects his compassion for those undergoing struggle and pain.

Similarly, Merrill Unger indicates that the word *peace* can have different scriptural meanings:

> The term is frequently found with reference to outward tranquillity thus relating to individuals, communities, and nations (Nm 6:26; 1 Sm 7:14; 1 Kgs 4:24; Acts 9:31). Another usage is that of Christian unity (Eph 4:3; 1 Thes 5:13). In its deepest application the word signifies a spiritual state, meaning a restored relationship with God and that which results from this relationship (Is 9:6–7; 26:3; 53:5; Ps 119:165; Lk 2:14; Jn 14:27; Acts 10:36; Rom 1:7; 5:1; Gal 5:22) (1957, 841).

> The peace offerings have their root in the state of grace with its
> fellowship with God. . . . They served to establish the Hebrew
> more firmly in the fellowship of divine grace. . . . The offerings
> also developed a conscious feeling of God's presence, especially
> during times of adversity (ibid., 948).

Christ informed his disciples that in him there is peace for the
troubled soul. He told them to expect tribulation, but that they
should "take courage" because he has conquered the world (Jn
16:33). Jesus said, "Peace I leave with you; my peace I give to you. I
do not give to you as the world gives. Do not let your hearts be troubled, and do not let them be afraid" (Jn 14:27). This promise is significant when we consider the peace offerings of the Hebrew
Scriptures. Israel's need for God's sustaining presence, so vividly
manifested in their peace offerings during times of difficulty, finds
fulfillment in Jesus Christ. Christ offers the peace of sustaining
grace. In fact, the prophet Isaiah spoke of one who would be called
the "Prince of Peace" (Is 9:6).

God promises peace to everyone who places their trust in him (Ps
29:11; Is 26:3), and this peace has eschatological truth (Is 2:3–5;
11:6–10; 54:10). The peace we experience in the present, which cul-
minates in the future, is made possible through the atonement of
Christ: "[He] was wounded for our transgressions, crushed for our
iniquities; upon him was the punishment that made us whole, and by
his bruises we are healed" (Is 53:5).

Paul tells us that the gospel message is one of peace: "To set the
mind on the flesh is death, but to set the mind on the spirit is life
and peace" (Rom 8:6; cf. Rom 10:15). He also explains that the
kingdom of God is "righteousness and peace and joy" (Rom 14:17)
in the Holy Spirit, and the fruit of the Spirit is "love, joy, [and]
peace" (Gal 5:22).

Christ's mission is to bring peace, "to give light to those who sit in
darkness" (Lk 1:79). Peace from the turmoil of sinful living becomes
a reality through God's forgiveness. Peace with God and others
brings an inner calm and provides us with the resources to work
through our trials.

The incarcerated need to understand that inner peace is a bond
with Jesus Christ that can be made even in a prison environment.
Paul's tribulations and incarceration are the prime examples of this

truth. The peace that Christ can give to prisoners will give them comfort and strength in the midst of turmoil.

Hope

Biblical hope finds its perfection in the future; however, the internalized Spirit provides hope in the present (1 Cor 9:24–27; 1 Thes 1:3). The writer of Hebrews was speaking of the present when he said, "We have this as a sure and steadfast anchor of the soul, a hope that enters into the inner shrine behind the curtain" (Heb 6:19). In the midst of weakness, there is a hope that strengthens us.

Most prisoners live with the hope of returning to society, but in Christ they can have eternal hope, the fruits of which begin while they are still in prison. Because the incarcerated live in God's forgiveness, they receive the Spirit of hope who bears witness to divine promises. The church cannot remove all the strife and pain from an individual's life, but it can be a continuing instrument of hope to carry people into God's perfect future.

Paradigms for Prison Ministry

The ministry of Jesus Christ reveals his identification with our situations, environments, and cultures. Jesus recognized that we must not care for only certain people, but rather for all living creatures. Regardless of the circumstances, Christ had the unique ability to place himself in another person's situation. As he explained to the Corinthians, Paul became all things to all people so that some of them might be won over to Christ (1 Cor 9:19–23).

Every ministry should conduct ongoing need assessments, particularly institutional ministries. The uniqueness of prison congregations necessitates special approaches to ministry. The emotional complexity and transitory aspects of prison life make the development of *paradigms* most important. Paradigms are church models that can be applied to all areas of ministry. They incorporate biblical subjects and themes that confront the obstacles of a particular environment to facilitate healing and personal development.

The isolation and punishment experienced by prisoners make it difficult for them to believe in divine forgiveness and grace. Therefore, the church must use models of ministry that address the feelings and beliefs that many felons share. The incarcerated live in a world that is altogether different than that of the free community, and chaplains must take this into consideration. The inmate stressors we examined in chapter 2 indicate the special needs found in penal institutions.

Felons seek a God who understands what they are going through, specifically their feelings of rejection, loneliness, and despair. Also, they need to see concrete evidence of grace flowing through the church. The unrelenting stress of prison makes it hard for them to realize that God is present and moves through them. For this reason, pertinent church models are important.

The following three paradigms—the dimensions of the cross, the ministry of presence, and the priesthood of servants—can benefit everyone. Yet, because of their unique situation, inmates identify with them in a special way.

The Dimensions of the Cross

The cross has a powerful attraction for convicted criminals. The Passion calls offenders to examine the life of Jesus Christ. Although our Lord's atonement holds many mysteries, it communicates penetrating images of God's involvement and identification with humanity. These images not only reveal the horror of sin but also encompass the human and divine feelings of a triune God.

Through the example of Christ at Calvary prisoners see a savior who experienced the legal system of his day. They follow the events that occurred after our Lord's arrest and, although his imprisonment was brief, they see that Christ is like them. Prisoners are drawn to a God who can truly identify with their plight. They can relate to a savior who understands their feelings of isolation and abandonment. Inmates gravitate toward Jesus because he knows the pain of being misunderstood, rejected by humanity, and seemingly forgotten by God.

The cross shows us a God who clearly understands human emotions and pain and from which we experience a divine compassion that is believable. As prisoners move toward the cross, they become consumed in a love that knows the extent of human adversity and the difficulties of a sinful world.

Forgiveness and Identification through Suffering

In the crucifixion of Jesus Christ we see the loving heart of a merciful God and learn the true meaning of love and the cost of forgiveness. As we listen to Jesus' cries and gaze upon his pierced body, we are assured that God knows both the pain of the flesh and the agony of the soul. This knowledge gives us comfort and strength, especially when we look beyond the grave to the empty tomb.

Isaiah's picture of the Suffering Servant speaks to our innermost being, for it depicts a "total emptying" for every sinner. The prophet tells us that Jesus "poured out himself to death, and was numbered with the transgressors; yet he bore the sin of many. . . ." (Is 53:12). In a selfless and sacrificial act, God gives us a savior who knows the full extent of our sins, pain, and sorrow and what it means to feel deserted and unloved. Isaiah's prophetic words tell us that Jesus too was familiar with suffering because he was despised, oppressed, and afflicted (Is 53:3–10). In other words, God was willing to do what was necessary for love. This is a powerful message for individuals who no longer feel the intimate affection of loved ones.

The Suffering Servant identifies with every aspect of our humanity. He wept over Jerusalem and at the death of Lazarus, and his compassion and power ushered a convicted criminal into Paradise. Jesus Christ bids all the imprisoned to come and receive the water of life (Rv 22:17).

God's Word emphasizes that there is no unforgivable sin, which takes us to Golgatha where sin and the cycle of revenge are conquered. When the cross is internalized, it gives proof of a divine grace that seeks out the darkest corners of sin, including those who are imprisoned for the most heinous crimes.

In the atonement of the cross, we find a God who stepped into history to sacrificially heal all who would respond in faith. According to Jurgen Moltmann, God takes humanity so seriously that he is willing to suffer under those he created.

> Jesus entered the company of the despised, the tortured, and the rejected. His public execution with two robbers can be interpreted as a sign of solidarity with these lost people As the community of the crucified Jesus we are drawn into his self-surrender, into his solidarity with the lost, and into his public suffering. His suffering is in this respect not exclusive but inclusive and leads to compassion (1975, 91–92).

Because Christ followed the path of suffering, we must reevaluate those who are spurned or avoided by society, including the destitute, sick, retarded, aged, and those who commit repulsive acts against society. Human infirmity and personal sin disturb us but as followers of Jesus, who was marred, Christians should reach out to everyone in need. Not only should we reach out to prisoners but also prisoners must minister to one another.

Inmates commonly claim that their peers are inferior. In Christ, however, we must communicate love to everyone, including the most repulsive people and those we perceive to be our enemies. When the church communicates this message of love, it participates in the Suffering Servant's conquest of sin and the affirmation of life. By sharing in Jesus' suffering on the cross, the church also shares in the redemptive work of Christ.

The cross reflects the reality of human hopelessness and our desperate need for grace. Ministry is understood and synthesized in Jesus' suffering on the cross, for it is here that the essence of God relates directly to humanity's predicament. The cross graphically speaks to sin and the slavery, guilt, and punishment that it brings. It also addresses oppression and injustice. Karl Barth notes that the "suffering, sin, abandonment, and peril (of those who were like sheep without a shepherd), not merely went to the heart of Jesus, but right into his heart, into Himself, so that their plight was now his own, and as such he saw and suffered it more keenly than they did" (1960a, 211). Jesus, who knew the sting of death, also lived the collective agonies of life.

Through Christ, God relates to all of our human infirmities, struggles, and losses. Not only did Jesus suffer physical and emotional trauma but also he bore the universal weight of sin. He accepted the anguish of every sin; thus identifying with the realities of all sinners. The cross offers an explanation of the revulsions and fears that so often cause people to act with cruelty or callous indifference toward others.

The incarcerated live with the suffering that comes from sin and, although Christ was without sin, inmates need to understand that their savior experienced the weight and divine wrath of every sin known to humanity. It is important for individuals who repeatedly resist God's grace and live under the torment and bondage of sin to remember this crucial point of theology.

Andrew Purves indicates that "because Jesus suffered as he did, and because he as God was wholly human, there is now no human suffering that is outside his lordship over suffering" (1989, 99). Similarly, in *The Crucified God*, Moltmann speaks about suffering and rejection:

To suffer and to be rejected are not identical. Suffering can be celebrated and admired. It can arouse compassion. But to be rejected takes away the dignity from suffering and makes it dishonorable suffering. To suffer and be rejected signify the cross (1974, 55).

Moltmann further explains God's suffering with these words:

In the forsakenness of the Son, the Father also forsakes himself. In the surrender of the Son, the Father also surrenders himself, though not in the same way. . . . The suffering and dying of the Son, forsaken by the Father, is a different kind of suffering from the suffering of the Father in the death of the Son. . . . To understand what happened between Jesus and his God and Father on the cross, it is necessary to talk in trinitarian terms. The Son suffers dying, the Father suffers the death of the Son. . . . The Fatherlessness of the Son is matched by the Sonlessness of the Father, and if God has constituted himself as the Father of Jesus Christ, then he also suffers the death of his Fatherhood in the death of the Son (ibid., 243).

Commenting on Moltmann's insights, Purves makes the claim that the death of Jesus is now part of the history between the Father and the Son, meaning that suffering and death are forever part of God's being. In essence, "God has been eternally changed by Jesus' incarnation into the vulnerability and contingency of the human condition" (1989, 73).

Dietrich Bonhoeffer wrote the following words shortly before his execution:

God lets himself be pushed out of the world on to the cross. He is weak and powerless in the world, and that is precisely the way, the only way, in which he is with us and helps us. Matthew 8:17 makes it clear that Christ helps us, not by virtue of his omnipotence, but by virtue of his weakness and suffering. . . . Only the suffering God can help. . . . That is a reversal of what the religious man expects from God. Man is summoned to share in God's suffering at the hands of a godless world (Moltmann 1974, 47).

Bonhoeffer's comments about Jesus' weakness and lack of power in this world bring an unusual theological twist. We tend to understand God in the context of omnipotence and, although his grace is certainly associated with his power, Bonhoeffer focuses on God's willful weakness and lack of power. The incarnation brought Christ to us as a suffering servant, and his wounds bond us to him. Not only does Jesus identify with our grief and pain, but we are drawn into his love. The cross assures us of God's compassionate understanding of the human struggle and condition, and this assurance gives comfort and strength to the weary and troubled soul.

Compared to their previous lives, prisoners find themselves in a weakened and powerless state in which they feel alone and unloved. But in Christ they have an advocate who understands the realities of human weakness and pain, and through his Spirit there is continuing strength. Even though Jesus willfully chose his plight, the emotional and spiritual implications of the cross do not change for us.

According to Moltmann,

> God brings help through his wounds. . . . Suffering is overcome by suffering, and wounds are healed by wounds. For the suffering in suffering is the lack of love, and the wounds in wounds are the abandonment, and the powerlessness in pain is unbelief. And therefore the suffering of abandonment is overcome by the suffering of love, which is not afraid of what is sick and ugly, but accepts it and takes it to itself in order to heal it. . . . Jesus was their identity (the enslaved) with God in a world which had taken all hope from them and destroyed their human identity until it was unrecognizable (ibid., 46, 48).

These insightful statements can bring healing and hope to the numerous prisoners who feel that their crimes have barred them from God's presence and mercy. Jesus Christ is not afraid of their sickness, and his very life gives them a new beginning. As Moltmann indicates, "They find in Jesus the brother who put off his divine form and took the form of a slave [Phil 2], to be with them and to love them" (ibid., 49).

The cross dispels ultimate fears, holds evil in check, confounds the powers of darkness, and makes it possible for us to identify with a God who made human experience his own. The following words communicate the beauty and power of the Lord's atonement:

God in Christ went all the way into our lostness and separation from God in order to restore us to a relationship with God. God in Christ, in Christ's compassionate atonement with us, entered into the depths of our sin and in becoming as we are, enabled us to become as he is (Purves 1989, 79, 80).

Those suffering from isolation, legal punishment, and extreme personal loss have difficulty relating to a deity who is removed from their situation. However, through Jesus Christ prison inmates not only relate to the humanity of God but also realize they need his help. They find solace in a divine presence that translates into sustaining and sanctifying grace. God's grace brings hope to persons who are experiencing the tensions of prison life. Only in the cross is there "courage in defeat and hope in the face of hopelessness" (Lettermann 1980, 156).

This theology does not promise easy victories or offer false security. Rather, it promises grace from a savior who relates to humanity through his own wounds. It also promises victory over sin, struggle, and death. Even though Isaiah's suffering servant was "struck down by God and afflicted," God's light in life is still guaranteed (Is 53:4, 11). Moltmann's words on this subject are penetrating:

Where lives have been deprived of freedom, dignity, and humanity, they find in fellowship with Christ respect, recognition, human dignity, and hope. This is a foothold and a freedom in faith which prevents those who suffer from abandoning themselves. . . . By becoming a friend of sinners and tax collectors, Jesus made their enemies his enemies. By claiming that God himself was on the side of the godless, he incited the devout against him and was cast out into the godlessness of Golgatha (1974, 49–51).

Participation in Divine Suffering
Thomas à Kempis encourages people to rest in Christ's Passion, finding in his sacred wounds the refuge that they so desperately need. He tells us that devout souls should and will feel, in all their troubles, a deep sense of consolation. Kempis's conclusions assure us that our movement toward the cross not only prevents us from belittling others but also allows us to bear criticisms (1966, 133). As we are drawn into the sufferings of Christ, we become one with God, which heals our wounds and brings us comfort and peace.

By meditation and adoration people have been drawn closer to the sufferings of Christ, participated in them and felt them as their own sufferings. And again, in their own sufferings, people have discovered a fellowship with the sacred head sore wounded. This spiritual absorption into the sufferings of Christ led, as late medieval mysticism said, to a conformity of the soul with the crucified Christ (Moltmann 1974, 45).

The incarcerated claim that the Eucharist is a special blessing to them. Many prisoners report that when they meditate on the wounds of Christ, they experience an emotional and spiritual bonding with God. Their experiences parallel the feelings of others who have prayerfully entered into an intimate fellowship with Christ. But prisoners seem to engage in deeper levels of meditation and thanksgiving than those who live in the free community. Their past lives and present circumstances influence their experience.

Participation in the Eucharist is a mystical, yet concrete, way of internalizing the suffering love of our Lord. Through silent meditation and reflective prayer, we experience a spiritual touching of Christ's wounds. Also, the broken bread and the wine enable us to probe our own brokenness and find strength in the power of the risen Christ. The Eucharist brings forgiveness through oneness with Jesus Christ.

Another dimension of the Eucharist is Christian unity, which is vividly communicated when individuals from different backgrounds come together to celebrate as members of one body. This mystical communion reveals that there is one Spirit and one church. In fact, only the Holy Spirit can bring together the multitude of differences that are found in humanity. This diversity, united through the one Spirit, manifests the creativity, beauty, and power of almighty God; and unity provides a strong witness of his transforming presence in the world.

The extremes found in prison communities make the Eucharist a crucial focus of ministry. In the fellowship of Holy Communion, there is a love and equality that tears down the many barriers that separate people. Through this sacrament we realize the power of diversity. Because the Eucharist exemplifies the diversity found in Jesus Christ, we come to understand that the church is a mystical communion that can only be made through the Spirit of Christ. This truth should lead us to examine our inner lives, which is yet another dimension of the cross.

Incarnation and the Cross

The serious nature of many offenses makes it difficult for felons to accept God's mercy. Their difficulty is reinforced by the unrelenting tensions of imprisonment—it is particularly difficult for those who are guilty of crimes that are abhorrent even to other prisoners. But Christ's sacrifice is offered to all people, regardless of their past lives, which includes even the most vicious criminals. The blood of Jesus Christ was shed for all sins, and his healing excludes no one. Only in the cross can prisoners receive total forgiveness and find hope for a new beginning. Chaplains must communicate this glorious message to every incarcerated person.

Criminal activity can never be condoned or rationalized, but the church should direct offenders toward a spirituality that encompasses all life experiences, including past sins, failed lifestyles, and imprisonment. Every situation allows for personal transformation, growth, and outreach to others. Whenever we think about giving up on others, we need to remember that God never gave up on us. Just as Christ reaches out in forgiveness and identifies with humanity through his own wounds, those who follow him must do the same. The cross draws us to God and sends us to others.

The Ministry of Presence

The church has a major role in correctional facilities, and its presence is vital to every inmate. It has a positive impact in these troubled communities, whether it is through the continuous visibility of the chapel or inmates interacting with a chaplain or Christian peers. Regardless of religious beliefs, the majority of felons view the church as a necessary and comforting presence. Prisoners need to see chaplains in the cell blocks, exercise yards, solitary housing units, and prison dispensaries. The closeness of the chaplain makes them feel that the church desires to be with them and cares about their welfare.

Some offenders view ministry as simply part of the penal system, but even these individuals prefer to take their problems to a chaplain or other spiritual representative. Generally speaking, inmates view the church as an element of stability in an unstable environment. As such, the church serves as a moral code and example of righteous living for both inmates and prison staff; it is an instrument of encouragement, support, and hope for everyone in the adverse environment of prison.

Need for a Pastoral Presence

Individuals experience pastoral care when someone reaches out to them in compassion. In the Garden of Gethsemane Jesus was deeply distressed. He was overwhelmed by sorrow, and so he asked his disciples to remain with him. Even though they could not understand his agony or change future events, their presence still comforted him (Mk 14:32–42).

The caring presence of another person during a time of trial can be healing. In a mysterious way, sharing our burdens with another person brings relief. Two people can form an emotional bond when the compassion is void of insensitive advice, theological rhetoric, criticism, and judgment. For example, Job's friends believed that they were engaged in ministry when the opposite was actually true. Their presence only aggravated an already devastating set of circumstances. Rather than identify with Job's suffering, they distanced themselves from his pain. Many well-intentioned people, including pastors and other care workers, often react this way.

A true friend is there when he or she is needed and has no agenda but to love and help mend wounds. Like the Good Samaritan, a friend responds as a caring physician. Following this example, we should be more concerned with others' pain than with their credentials or the reasons for their predicament.

People who are in pain need a pastoral presence, mostly because suffering brings profound feelings of isolation and abandonment. Christ's feeling that God had abandoned him at Golgatha caused him to cry out in excruciating pain, "My God, my God, why have you forsaken me?" (Mk 15:34). In fact, presence is so important that Jesus promises never to abandon or forsake us: "I am with you always, to the end of the age" (Mt 28:20). God has chosen to share our struggles, and biblical history reinforces this truth. Jurgen Moltmann writes that

> God himself cuts himself off from himself, giving himself away to his people, suffering with their sufferings, going with them into the misery of the foreign land, wandering with their wanderings. . . . God himself, in that he sells himself to Israel—and what should be more natural for God our Father! and suffers its fate with it, makes himself in need of redemption. In this way, in this suffering the relationship between God and the remnant points beyond itself (1975, 61).

God's presence is at his own initiative, involving extreme sacrifice. This same ministry of initiative and sacrifice belongs to the church. Christian ministry must be an intentional and sensitive presence that makes a difference through caring and the willingness to share and expose itself. The involvement of the church is not exercised from a distance or in an obligatory way, but through a love that seeks out human need and suffering. According to Karl Barth:

> The concept of God as a "wholly other" does not reflect the deity of Abraham, Isaac, and Jacob. . . . God does not act in a vacuum as a divine being-for-Himself. Instead, He exists, speaks, and acts as the partner of man, possessing the character of the humanity which He created. It is precisely God's deity which, rightly understood, includes his humanity. . . . In Jesus Christ there is no isolation of man from God or of God from man. Jesus Christ is in His one Person, as true God, man's loyal partner, as true man, God's. He is the Lord humbled for communion with man and likewise the Servant exalted to communion with God. . . . In this oneness Jesus is the Mediator and Reconciler between God and man who comes to man on behalf of God to awaken faith, love, and hope (1960b, 45–47).

For the church to make a difference in a world full of contradictions and trials, the ministry of presence must be revitalized. But presence can only be experienced if the church moves beyond fixed structures and the realm of self, touching people where they are in life. Like Christ, we must eat with life's prisoners so that they might know and experience the transforming love of God. Sanctification should never be understood as separation from the diseases and struggles of humanity. The truly sanctified church must recognize that only sensitivity and compassion bring healing, creating an intentional ministry that is void of complacency, indifference, and self-interest.

As God's salt, the church cannot remain in a state of contentment and idleness while oppression and suffering abound. Rather, the church must prayerfully shake its existing structures, penetrating the unpleasant segments of society—including penal institutions. Far from being an idealistic, superficial, or mechanical change, it is a conversion to the realization that ministry is found even in the most offensive places. This ministry includes an active listening to the nonverbal cries of the oppressed and rejected, which allows us to commune with the depths of reality, and thus share in what God experiences. The church must realize that its mission is more than proclamation in words.

Jesus reminds us that ministry to the least is ministry to him, and this takes the church into all the prisons of life (Mt 25:35–46). Christ's mission is to tell us that we must move beyond our comfortable and secure surroundings to understand and meet the needs of other people. The ministry of presence penetrates the walls of separation caused by prejudice, mistrust, anger, and fear. This front-line pastoral care responds to both spoken and silent calls for help. The church is not simply an organization, but a movement into and through the world, sustained by the Spirit who works through the apostolate and the priesthood of believers.

Moltmann writes the following about the dimensions of Christ's presence:

> Christ, by virtue of his identifying assurance is present in the apostolate, in baptism, in the Lord's supper, and in the fellowship of the brethren. This is a Real Presence in the Spirit through identification, and an identification on the basis of promise (1975, 125).

Based on these truths, it is important that the church project a presence that draws people to God's fellowship where divine grace is dispensed in transforming and sustaining ways. The church should be experiential, touching the lives of others concretely. As the embodiment of Christ, the church should reflect a sacrificial and practical servanthood whose healing elements bring comfort and hope.

Like the ministry of the Good Samaritan, the priesthood should not be afraid to reach out to those who are different and walk in their misfortune. This ministry of faith should accept God's call to the undesirable, the morally diseased, and the forgotten segments of society. In essence, Christian ministry must be a visible and involved conscience that is patterned after the life of Christ in order to bring healing and life to the sick and those who are motivated by evil.

In his essay titled "Christ the Healer," Roland Miller provides the following thoughts:

> God enters the sphere of evil, draws near to it, yes even becomes identified with evil in order to overcome it (2 Cor 5:21). This is

the "unnatural" thing for God to do. There is strain in it. There is
suffering in it. So God who naturally recoils from evil sends himself. The Son of Love who would naturally go must nevertheless
be sent into the arena of the evil one. It is evident that it was this
sense of being sent by the Father that enabled Jesus Christ to
maintain his commitment in his traumatic and unnatural
encounter with evil and suffering. "Oh my Father, if it be possible, let this cup pass from me: nevertheless not as I will, but as
thou wilt. . . . Oh my Father, if this cup may not pass from me I
drink it, thy will be done" (Mt 26:39, 42). The Sent One drank
the cup. Goodness engaged with evil in mortal combat, and in
that battle death is swallowed up in victory.

Even so Christ the Healer sends us. He sends us to the
unnatural thing, to be in contact with evil, to be involved with
sickness and suffering. He commends us to heal. He knows
that we require a commission, and he gives it. We do not only
love, but we are sent to love. . . . Only those who believe that
they have been sent by God to do battle with evil will be able
to drink the cup that he drank, and to give as they have
received (1980, 21).

A ministry of presence does not condemn, nor does it necessarily
give advice or demand to know the reasons for an individual's circumstances. Such a presence is only concerned with the alleviation
of suffering. While it certainly confronts sin, it does so in the spirit
of Christ's love, as a compassionate healer rather than as a judge.

When the body of Christ visibly serves the people of the community, it has a strong influence upon the "would-be" actions of people,
and thus prevents sin and suffering.

Presence Exemplified in Christ
Roland Miller (1980, 29–31) reveals some pertinent applications for
Christ's ministry of presence:

He noticed.
Jesus was alert, actually seeking out those in need (Jn 5:16).
He stopped.
Jesus did not simply pass by those who were suffering; he
responded to what he saw (Mt 20:32).

He was horrified.
> Jesus was horrified at what he saw, for the suffering and sad-
> ness he encountered was not God's intention. Humanity, how-
> ever, has lost its sense of horror. We have seen too much, so
> what we see no longer moves us (Mk 7:34).

He was angry.
> Jesus hated everything that distorted God's objectives, includ-
> ing the self-righteous who could not see God's priorities of
> forgiveness and human need (Mt 21:12; 23:23).

He loved.
> There was profound intimacy and hope in Jesus' love. In
> Christ we see God's tears for his children (Mt 8:3, 7; 14:14; Jn
> 11:3, 33–34).

He loved widely, yet personally
> Jesus did not love from a distance but, rather, in personal and
> concrete forms (Mt 19:2; 20:34).

He healed relevantly.
> Christ kept in touch with our culture and healed understand-
> ably (Mt 8:4).

He crossed lines.
> Jesus was truly the man for others, and this truth still causes
> people to wonder (Mt 5:44; 8:11; Mk 7:29).

He healed as a servant.
> Christ rejected all forms of worldly power and acclaim. He
> deliberately withdrew from the popular results of his healing
> activity (Mt 12:16; 20:28; Jn 6:15).

He was urgent.
> Jesus revealed a sense of little time, realizing that night was
> coming. He said, "My Father is still working, and I also am
> working" (Jn 5:17).

Like Christ, the church must be alert to the cries of humanity and
not simply observe from a distance. Jesus was horrified and angry at
what he encountered, and so must the church be horrified and
angry. The church must never become insensitive or fatalistic,
believing any situation is hopeless. Instead, the church's presence, as
exemplified in Christ, must refuse to accept that human pain is
inevitable. The church is called to be a servant of urgency, reaching
out and touching those deemed incurable.

But the mission of the priesthood requires personal wounding, struggle, and the death of self. The church must meet others where they are in life, including the emotionally disturbed, the physically sick, and those who are filled with hatred and anger. Identifying with such persons often results in emotional and spiritual exhaustion and loneliness from being misunderstood by those who cast aside the unappealing. Many people, including those who profess to be Christians, cannot comprehend that there can be ministry to individuals who have committed certain crimes.

A ministry of presence means we must help others in their pain. In essence, we should offer pastoral care in whatever form is needed so that others can have a transforming encounter with the risen Christ. We must give to others the grace that has been given to us.

An Example of Pastoral Care
John Keble, an Anglican clergyman, worked for the causes of the Oxford Movement in the 1830s. The movement rebelled against a growing liberalism inside and outside the church, primarily among the clergy. Keble faithfully worked to restore the church traditions that were dispensed with at the time of the Reformation. Like other Oxford reformers, he was concerned about incorporating the love of God in his ministry. In other words, rather than merely being a professional pastor, Keble wanted to bring the presence of God to the lives of the people (Stone 1989, 2–3).

In an article titled "The Pastoral Care of John Keble, Oxford Reformer," Howard Stone (1989) sets forth Keble's approach to pastoral care. Stone highlights insights from Keble's letters that are significant when we consider the ministry of presence. While ministry means giving support to others, John Keble also believed that there are times when biblical instruction is essential because the Scriptures address human lifestyles and cannot be separated from love for others.

Keble was accessible to people. He believed that persons in need take precedence over other pastoral duties. His interactions with people reveal his sensitivity to personal uniqueness and special circumstances. Keble's own sense of unworthiness and empathy toward others helped to create a ministry of humility. He viewed pastors as servants and clearly exemplified this role in his daily life (ibid., 6–7).

Keble also gave instruction and confronted sin when the Spirit led him to do so. He instructed people to love God through their actions, even if God's presence and care are not personally experienced. He indicated that we cannot always control our feelings, but we can control our actions. Keble told parishioners not to doubt God's forgiveness but trust that it is there even when it is not felt. His response to suffering stressed two points: *we can benefit from suffering* and *Christ is with us*. He believed that suffering helps us develop character, and that in some mysterious way our bodily sufferings are united to those of our Lord on the cross (ibid., 12–13). We can identify with Jesus Christ through our own trials and suffering.

Keble responded to the sins of others quite seriously. He feared the consequences of not speaking out, even to friends, if he believed a person's conduct was improper. He felt that believers need to recognize their sin, face it, confess it, and amend their lives. But even when he confronted sin, he did it in the gentle spirit of Christian love. Regardless of the situation, he always communicated a servant's humility (ibid., 13–14). When we consider the ministry of presence, humility must always be emphasized.

John Keble's example of pastoral care is helpful to prison ministry. Providing an accessible presence of servanthood that addresses the uniqueness of people and their circumstances is vital in the penal setting. Also, in a prison community where positive feelings are difficult to maintain, an emphasis on faith over emotions is important. Prisoners need disciplined behavior that promotes positive responses. While suffering must be understood as an inescapable reality, it should nonetheless be properly communicated as an identification and bonding with Christ. It can then be experienced as the foreshadowing of God's ultimate victory.

While Keble's approach to sin is important to all ministry, it is especially significant in correctional facilities. The lives of many inmates reveal years of distorted thinking, bitter attitudes, and crime—sometimes since early childhood. Frequently, an individual's behavior is never seriously confronted until his or her arrest and imprisonment.

Even though God's presence is one of perfect love, sin cannot be rationalized. Therefore, the church must preach repentance and faith as the necessary vehicles for forgiveness and a changed life. A positive presence can only be maintained when the church refuses to grant a waiver concerning sin. Spiritual compromises that take place in prison increase the power of evil in a community that is already engulfed in destructive forces.

The Essence of Presence

The ministry of presence can be summed up in the word *compassion:* "[Jesus] had compassion for them, because they were like sheep without a shepherd" (Mk 6:34). How do we interpret the compassion of our Lord? Compassion is not simply mercy, empathy, sympathy, or pity; instead, "compassion is a feature of our being in Christ. It is not an ethical or psychological disposition, something to have now and then, as we allow our hearts to be warmed on occasion in concern for another" (Purves 1989, 41).

In his book *The Search for Compassion,* Andrew Purves offers the following images:

> Compassion is conventionally defined as suffering with another person. . . . In its soteriological dimension, however, compassion means not only "suffering with another" but also "suffering for another." In compassion, one may carry the sin and suffering of others in such a way that they may be restored to wholeness precisely because their sin and suffering are borne. One's compassionate solidarity with the suffering of another becomes a redemptive solidarity. It is an entry into another's lostness, displacement, and separation. And because of the journey of the compassionate one into the far country of another's lostness, through compassion and suffering, a redemptive bond is established which can bring that other home (ibid., 55).

> Compassion asks us to go where it hurts, to enter places of pain, to share in brokenness, fear, confusion and anguish. Compassion challenges us to cry out with those in misery, to mourn with those who are lonely, to weep with those in tears. Compassion requires us to be weak with the weak, vulnerable with the vulnerable, and powerless with the powerless. Compassion means full immersion in the condition of being human.
>
> Here we see what compassion means. It is not bending toward the underprivileged from a privileged position; it is not a reaching out from on high to those who are less fortunate below; it is not a gesture of sympathy or pity for those who fail to make it in the upward pull. On the contrary, compassion means going directly to those people and places where suffering is most acute and building a home there (ibid., 35).

No other insights and truths could be more applicable to prison ministry than these. Representing Christ in penal institutions unquestionably involves identification with others at the deepest levels possible. Ministering to prisoners truly means "building a home" in the midst of acute suffering. This type of pastoral care requires patient tolerance to confront the anger and aggression of individuals who are considered to be incorrigible and unworthy of mercy. The ministry of the church should penetrate these dark and dangerous crevices of life with the message of forgiveness and hope.

The ministry of compassionate presence is "pain borne and tears shed in order that another may carry a lighter load" (Purves 1989, 131). Grace is received and then given to others, sometimes in an unorthodox and misunderstood fashion. But somehow "we must show to others the mercy we have ourselves received from God. We cannot stand on our rights, for then God will stand on God's rights and the sentence that is rightly ours will be pronounced. Who could be saved then?" (ibid., 43).

Jesus' association with society's outcasts brought him stern criticism (Mt 11:19), but this vulnerability to criticism is the path of righteousness. The church is not called to appease the self-righteousness and sinful appetites of scoffers, including the rich and powerful, but to serve those for whom Jesus died. Jesus shared these words of truth:

> For I was hungry and you gave me food, I was thirsty and you gave me something to drink, I was a stranger and you welcomed me, I was naked and you gave me clothing, I was sick and you took care of me, I was in prison and you visited me. . . . Truly, I tell you, just as you did it to one of the least of these who are members of my family, you did it to me (Mt 25:35–36, 40).

Presence as Example

In the final analysis, presence is an example for Christians, as in all environments, but it is especially essential in prison. Providing an example for Christian living not only stimulates the personal growth of inmates but also serves as a strong witness to the prison community and, in turn, draws prisoners to Christ and the church.

The apostle Paul believed that a Christ-like presence was crucial to evangelism. He points to the living example of Christ's humility, servanthood, and sacrifice on our behalf. Jesus performed many acts of mercy to provide an example for his disciples: "So if I, your Lord and Teacher, have washed your feet, you also ought to wash one another's feet. For I have set you an example, that you also should do as I have done to you" (Jn 13:16–17). As the extension of Jesus Christ, human lives should be holy examples of God's infinite love and transforming grace. Those who are in Christ will draw others to his saving and sustaining grace.

Paul told Timothy that he could overcome his immaturity by setting an example in speech, conduct, love, faith, and purity (1 Tm 4:12). In addition, Paul gives examples of evil and how we should learn from their messages. He alludes to the Israelites and how their lives brought divine judgment: "Now these things occurred as examples, to keep us from setting our hearts on evil things as they did" (1 Cor 10:6). Our example before others reflects who we are. Our influence must never be understated.

Prisoners continuously search for something that will give meaning and new direction to their lives. In their quest, many of them investigate different religions and examine the attitudes and behavior of those who participate in these religions. In correctional facilities, inmates observe Christians more than any other group. They want to ascertain if Christians are different: whether they really have inner peace, spiritual strength, and love. Therefore, the church must develop a strong priesthood in prison communities. Christian inmates are the primary communicators of the gospel and the main support system for their peers.

A Pastoral Presence in Prison

Prison chaplains must engage with others at the feeling level and understand all people as equals, rather than aspire to be skilled professionals who can manipulate the lives of others for their good. Their presence should reflect a compassion that is made possible through their own sins and wounds. In other words, a chaplain's imperfections and need for continuing grace enables him or her to be compassionate toward others. As John Keble indicated, our imperfections make humility possible. All of our experiences, when transformed by God's love, can be ministry to other people (Pattison 1988, 140, 151, 152).

For others to see Christ, chaplains must mirror his essence. Such a presence testifies to both the reality of God and his love for humanity. It is also evidence that no sin is outside the scope of God's forgiveness. In whatever form, the ministry of presence must be an encounter with the spirit of Jesus Christ, which can only be realized through prayerful seeking and serving.

Priesthood of Servants

An active priesthood provides inmates with encouragement and support that would not otherwise be possible in prison. Yet, many offenders have difficulty understanding how they can be useful in their surroundings. It is common for inmates to view themselves as needy, rather than as individuals who can minister to others. While this feeling is understandable, the task of the church is to bring all people into the priesthood of God, including the incarcerated.

The priesthood brings renewed life to prison ministry and the inmate community. The numerous needs of offenders, combined with the limitations placed on clergy, make the priesthood indispensable in prison. It transforms a lifeless structure into an organism that lives and moves through the power of the Holy Spirit. Through the priesthood inmates can experience a fellowship of love and mutual support.

In prison, as elsewhere, the essential component of the priesthood is the humble servanthood that is clearly exemplified in Christ. This service is motivated by love and carried through in the spirit of humility. The prophet Isaiah revealed that the Messiah would be a humble servant whose power reflects a gentle spirit and offers hope for those imprisoned by sin and oppression (Is 42:1–7). In other words, the priesthood comprises those who have been spiritually regenerated and are bonded to Christ and one another through the inner life of the Spirit.

Eugene Peterson says the following about Christ's servanthood:

The servant role was completed in Jesus. Though there were auspicious signs that preceded and accompanied his birth, preparing the world for the majestic and kingly, the birth of Jesus itself was of the humblest peasant parentage, in an unimportant town, and in the roughest of buildings. He made a career of rejecting marks of status or privilege: he touched lepers, washed the feet of his disciples, befriended little children, encouraged women to join his entourage, and finally, submitted to crucifixion by a foreign power (1980, 181).

Avery Dulles clarifies Jesus' mission with these thoughts:

> Jesus is the servant who came not only to proclaim the coming
> of the kingdom, but also to give himself for its realization. He
> came to serve, to heal, to reconcile, to bind up wounds. Jesus,
> we may say, is in an exceptional way the Good Samaritan. He is
> the one who comes alongside of us in our need and in our sor-
> row, extending himself for our sake. . . . (1974, 92).

The Priesthood as an Extension of Christ

The priesthood of believers is the presence of Christ in action—people reaching out to others with concrete forms of service. The priesthood is the extension of Christ the healer—those who are willing to
suffer in order to help alleviate the pain of others. According to
Bonhoeffer, "The Church is only the Church when it lives in someone else's house, not its own" (Dulles 1974, 94, 96). The writers of
the Christian Scriptures confirmed this belief when they spoke
about the gifts of the Spirit. Everything they communicated pertains
to ministry within the scope of community life, rather than simply
for one's own benefit (Johnson 1989, 74).

Christ came into the world to put our spirituality into perspective.
Mother Teresa says that

> God has identified himself with the hungry, the sick, the naked,
> the homeless; hunger not only for bread, but for love, for care,
> to be somebody to someone; nakedness, not of clothing only,
> but nakedness of that compassion that very few people give to
> the unknown; homelessness, not just for shelter made of stone,
> but that homelessness that comes from having no one to call
> your own (ibid., 46).

Susanne Johnson writes that "Christ teaches us how to live for
others (Phil 2:4–5), telling us that when we prove ourselves neighbors in a radical fashion, we are not far from the kingdom of God
(Mk 12:23)" (ibid., 47). This message is vital for prisoners who are
disconnected from mainstream society. If they are separated from
the priesthood, it is hard for inmates to see the work of the Spirit.

Disciples of Christ are called to a "foot-washing" experience,
which requires a humble and serving spirit. Christians cannot forget
that "the Son of Man came not to be served, but to serve, and to give

his life a ransom for many" (Mk 10:45). This statement seals the truth that those who seek to save their lives will lose them (Mk 10:39).

Moltmann reminds us that "the one to whom all authority was given in heaven and on earth, emptied himself even unto death on a cross" (1975, 103). Any ministry that strays from this focus forsakes the Christ who died for the healing and reconciliation of all people. In this horizontal mission, in which we serve one another, the church meets the personhood of Christ. Jesus said, "Truly I tell you, just as you did it to one of the least of these who are members of my family, you did it to me" (Mt 25:40). As Moltmann indicates, "the Church can only be apostolic when it takes up its cross. Its apostolic succession is the succession of the suffering Christ" (1975, 361). Being bound to God, we are also bound to those in need. Here lies true freedom and the fulfillment of the law (1 Cor 9:19; Gal 5:13; 6:2). But as emphasized by Hans Küng,

> It is not just a question of voluntary external self-abasement, as practiced on certain days of the year by leaders of some communities, but a total existence in a life and death of service for others as prefigured by the service of Jesus himself (Mt 20:28; Mk 10:45) and as demanded by Jesus of those who would serve him. . . . (1976, 501).

These are pertinent statements, and they demand examination because they define the purpose for our being, making clear distinctions between the church and other institutions. Bonhoeffer's (1963) symbol of Jesus as the "Man for Others" requires deep reflection, both individually and collectively as the body of Christ.

As members of the church, inmates must be taught that they are valuable in God's kingdom. They need to see their environment as a mission field, recognizing that they reside in a community that is accessible to few outside Christian workers. Prisoners should be encouraged to move beyond their own pain in order to touch the lives of those around them. In this way, prisoners not only minister to other people, but their actions become a channel of grace for them. Any ministry that only addresses individuals without emphasizing the need for community nurturing and mutual healing will never be strong, and in time it will fade away.

In every penal institution there are individuals with special gifts that, when developed, can be a blessing to others. No one can identify better with prisoners than their peers, and those who have been spiritually transformed are unquestionably the most effective communicators of the gospel and witnesses of the new life in Christ. Felons do not doubt the lifestyles of clergy and Christian volunteers who come into institutions, but they are suspicious of their fellow inmates. Therefore, when their peers have undoubtedly changed, inmates are able to vividly see and believe in the power of God. Inmate witness is a source of strength and hope, and a good Christian example.

On Mount Sinai God told his chosen people that they would be "a priestly kingdom and a holy nation" (Ex 19:6). In accordance with that promise, the Spirit has been poured out to all believers, granting gifts of ministry for serving humanity in supportive and sacrificial ways. Paul affirms God's promise by telling us to carry each other's burdens (Gal 6:2). Bruce Birch and Larry Rasmussen remind us that "radical love and a caring justice are not optional acts of voluntary piety; they are at the heart of what it means to be a people of God" (1989, 28).

The servanthood of Christ manifested God's love in concrete and practical forms, breaking down the barriers of prejudice and hatred. Jesus came for the sick and dying, including the worst cases in the most difficult environments. His servanthood made no distinctions. This message is for all humanity to hear.

Ministry in prison can only be successful when the believers become part of a priesthood, touching one another's lives with a sensitive presence of compassion and support. By participating in such a ministry we heal others, and at the same time heal ourselves. Ministry to other people has a miraculous way of alleviating our own pain, which applies directly to the daily needs of prisoners. Hans Küng confirms this idea with these words:

> Each person is responsible for his fellow men, called to share in his struggles and in his difficulties, called to bear his sins with him and to stand by him in everything. The priesthood is a fellowship in which each Christian, instead of living for himself, lives before God for others and is in turn supported by others. . . . (1976, 487).

The priesthood in prison should reflect service to one another with practical implementation. In essence, it should be an active and visible outreach through intercessory prayer groups, contacts with new inmates and those with serious needs, small cell block Bible studies, the sharing of Christian literature, or informal fellowships for mutual support. Again, it is important that the priesthood maintain a servant's spirit and engage in intentional ministry. It is easy to call the church a priesthood, but without an attitude of service, it means nothing to those in need.

Inmates must be encouraged to support one another in nonjudgmental ways; that is, to rejoice in the "otherness" of their peers. Their purpose must always be to increase their love for God and their neighbor (Niebuhr 1956, 39). The fundamental nature of servanthood—serving God and humanity—is the church in its pure state. The church must keep its focus on Jesus Christ by not abandoning him as our first love and purpose for being (Rv 2:4). Thus, prison ministry must include every believer, and the motivation for all its actions should be the will and love of almighty God.

In *The Beauty of Caring*, Lloyd John Ogilvie (1981, 32–33) shares his thoughts on what it means to be a servant. He lists five important elements:

We are impelled.
Because our own needs have been met by Christ, we are impelled to help others in need.

We identify.
Servants do not serve from a safe distance; they feel the pain and suffering of another as if it were their own. When God came to us through Christ, he did not give lofty advice, he became one of us.

We intercede.
Prayers of intervention not only unleash the power of God in another person's life but also clarify what the Lord wants us to say to that person. The intensity of our caring must be focused so that it meets the person's deepest need.

We are involved.
We must listen to others and dare to enter their situations. It is easy to tell others what to do, but it is difficult to get inside their skin and feel their anguish, fear, or frustration. People need to feel an intense empathy.

We are incisive in introducing people to the Savior.
Many people help others with physical or emotional suffering, but leave them with an eternal problem. As servants, we must also help people heal spiritually.

Through his identification with our infirmities and struggles, Christ qualifies as our high priest. His ministry was not merely observation but an involvement that has eschatological implications (Jn 12:26; 14:2; 17:24; 20:17). As Karl Barth states, "Jesus is wholly the Good Samaritan whose example demands that we go and do likewise. Humanity was created to be God's covenant-partner, and this means serving one another in diligence and love" (1960a, 203, 210). Barth offers a glimpse of the divine essence that motivates the servanthood of Christ:

> The private life of Jesus can never be an autonomous theme in the New Testament. This is true even of his private life with God. The Johannine discourses contain extensive expositions of the relationship of the Father to the Son and the Son to the Father, but they do not attribute any independent aim to this relationship. In the strict sense, they do not stand alone, but tirelessly aim to show that Jesus is for others, near and distant, disciples, Israel and the world, and to show what he is for them, for man. What he is in his relationship as the Son to the Father is not something which he is and has for himself. He does not experience or enjoy it as a private religious person. He is it as a public person (ibid., 209).

Luke records that Jesus sent his disciples out to preach the kingdom of God and to heal the sick (Lk 9:2). This is the same commission given to every follower of Christ and to every community. Jesus said, "As the Father has sent me, so I send you" (Jn 20:21). Henry Lettermann writes,

> The community of God's people is a broken community, living in a broken world. But at the same time it is a healed and healing community. This brokenness, which yearns for healing, is both individual and corporate. Tragically, we know the effects of brokenness, such as injury, disease, and incapacity, conflict and tension with self and others, pollution and abuse, threat of war and calamities, imprisonment by racism and disenfranchisement, and imposed philosophies and life styles. Healing in this life is never complete. Yet, paradoxically, wholeness of life is experienced in the midst of pain and suffering. Those who suffer can lay claim to healing in spite of their infirmities,

through the peace which comes from God and through those who love, care, and support (1980, 150).

Joel Hempel and Jill Westberg offer specific aspects of Christian care, all of which find application in community life (1980, 120–22). While incarceration may necessitate some modifications, these themes are helpful in comprehending the collective potential of ministry in a group setting. The following areas of ministry have a special impact in prisons, where the church has clear limitations, particularly in areas of social ministry.

Being present
> We must give our body, mind, feelings, senses, and spirituality.

Giving our time
> The quality of our time is important. It is difficult for us to be caring when we are preoccupied with our own schedule and agenda.

Listening
> To hear others, we have to involve all our senses. We must pay attention to words, body language, affect, avoidances, wants, needs, values, problems, and resistance.

Sharing
> We must be free to reveal our likes, dislikes, fears, struggles, strengths, and weaknesses. This capability also brings ministry to ourselves.

Confronting
> We must speak the truth in the spirit of love (Eph 4:15).

Supporting
> We should help others in their struggle. Empathizing with them assures them of their value.

Providing religious resources
> Religious resources include prayer, confession, congregational gifts, and the sacraments.

Clarifying facts and determining options
> We must help people determine what can be changed in their lives. This is especially important when we are working with people who are overwhelmed by their problems.

Jesus taught that human beings are the keepers of their brothers and sisters, meaning that we have a mutual obligation to and responsibility for one another. We can view Jesus' command to reach out to the less fortunate in a community context. The parable of the Good Samaritan points out that the word *neighbor* is not determined by geography or race. Rather, Christians should touch the lives of all people, understanding that *community* and *humanity* have the same meaning.

A person's worth must never be categorized or prioritized according to race, socioeconomic standing, or behavior. Rather, the church calls us to see others solely in terms of their needs and to respond to those needs in the best way possible. Niebuhr suggests that the "basic guideline for making ethical choices is to ask what the loving thing is to do" (Stivers et al. 1989, 234).

Interestingly, Lamentations was written in the context of community. Eugene Peterson provides us with some noteworthy points:

> When biblical people wept, they wept with their friends. . . . The biblical way to deal with suffering is to transform what is individual into something corporate. . . . Response to suffering is a function of the congregation. . . . Most cultures show a spontaneous comprehension of this. The suffering person is joined by friends who come together in a communal lament. They do not hush up the sound of weeping but augment it. They do not hide the sufferer away from view of everyone. . . . When others join the sufferer, there is consensual validation that the suffering means something. . . . When suffering cannot be expressed emotionally, there is a consequent inability to recover. . . . Further, community participation insures a human environment (1980, 114–15).

According to Peterson, the community allows people to enter the invisible company of those who have had the same or similar struggles and have survived. This contact permits the expression of emotions, the results of which are healing and the restoration of humanity (ibid., 116). These are important truths for prisoners who share similar frustrations, loss, and dehumanization. The penal community can be a supportive and healing priesthood through the mystical presence of Christ. When the priesthood of presence is a reality, inmates grow spiritually and find that they can serve others even in the confinement of the prison setting.

Most biblical images of religious identity are related to community life; for example, the Bible presents images of Israel as a family, a kingdom, a covenant, a banquet, one vine with many branches, a body with many parts, a chosen race, and a royal priesthood (Birch and Rasmussen 1989, 26–27). Peterson states that the biblical view of humanity is "person-in-community"—a people of God. He writes that

> The essential reality of humanity is corporate. . . . Adam was not complete until there was Eve. The meaning is clear: no individual is complete in himself, in herself; humanity is person-in-relationship. Persons are always part of community even when they deny it, even when they don't know it (1980, 154).

If community is a fact of life in both the church and society, then an obvious question must be asked: What kind of community are we? Ministry does not become a reality simply because we desire it or because it has organizational structure. To become a priesthood, we must have the "mystical" presence of Jesus Christ, which is only possible when the church receives grace and lives a life of faith.

The Priesthood as a United Body

The personal and environmental extremes found in prison frequently translate into conflict and division. The church is not exempt from these negative energies. Even spiritually advanced inmates struggle to understand the scope of biblical unity, with its ecumenical and eschatological significance. The tensions found in prison produce a climate that makes Christian unity difficult to achieve and maintain. Negative attitudes resulting from anger and suspicion stifle the spiritual growth that brings people together.

God's loving acceptance of people in their "otherness" is therefore a message that needs to be stressed. An understanding of unity within the church provides felons with an all-inclusive God who accepts them regardless of their past sins and present imperfections. Their inclusion then calls them to move beyond the bounds of narrow thinking and experience a multiform God whose creativity reflects diversity. This sense of God flows into their relationships and other aspects of their lives, uniting all people under one banner. Such unity leads to a strong evangelistic witness and an undivided crusade against evil.

The Source and Cost of Unity

Christian unity has its human beginnings in the triune God who separated and emptied himself to bring life to fallen humanity. Like a loving parent who suffers radical surgery to give a vital organ to a dying child, so it is with God who gave himself that humanity might live in wholeness.

The cost of unity is found in the divine sacrifice of separation and death. For humanity to be united with God and one another, separation and death within the Trinity was necessary. Unity is made possible through God's experience of abandonment, isolation, and death. The unity that developed through God's initiative and pain is a reality that surpasses time and boundaries, drawing all people to Christ. For unity God became man, and Christ died. Now, through the power of the risen Christ, the church is one body and one life with Jesus Christ as its head.

The church is called to be a fellowship of compassion and tolerance, a community where members can experience acceptance and self-worth. But this is only possible as people increase in love for God and their neighbors. H. Richard Niebuhr tells us that "the increase of love of God and neighbor remains the purpose and hope of our preaching the gospel, of all our Church organization and activity, of all our ministry, of all our efforts to train individuals for the ministry" (1956, 39).

The wounds of our Lord forever communicate the inclusiveness and cost of ministry. The impact of God's healing power is realized by others through a sacrificial giving that sets aside everything that hinders restoration. The following statement of the Seventh-day Adventist Church is a summary of biblical truths.

> The Church is one body with many members, called from every nation, kindred, tongue, and people. In Christ we are a new creation; distinctions of race, culture, learning, nationality, and differences between high and low, rich and poor, males and females, must not be divisive among us. We are all equal in Christ, who by one Spirit has bonded us into one fellowship with Him and with one another; we are to serve and be served without partiality or reservation. Through the revelation of Jesus Christ in the Scriptures we share the same faith and hope, and reach out in one witness to all. This unity has its source in the oneness of the triune God, who has adopted us as His children (Ministerial Association 1988, 170).

As Christ completed his work, even as he faced death, he contemplated the lives of his disciples in the context of unifying love. In

Gethsemane Jesus was concerned about the unity of his followers, wanting them to have a oneness in love and purpose like the unity of the Trinity: "As you, Father, are in me and I am in you, may they also be in us" (Jn 17:21). Jesus explained that humility was the substance of discipleship, and that true followers would be servants of God. In fact, the greatest in the kingdom would be the servant of all (Mk 10:35–45). But Jesus' words, like his example of the foot washing (Jn 13:5–17), appeared to fall on deaf ears.

Instead of transcending this world and becoming otherworldly, Christians tend to become enmeshed in a superficial ministry that is void of God's unifying love. Like the congregation in Ephesus (Acts 19), the church often forsakes the foundation upon which all ministry is built. Sin wears many faces, but its root is lack of knowing Christ's love in our hearts.

Not comprehending God's love, the disciples were sometimes motivated by ego, jealousy, legalism, and prejudice. It is little wonder that they were shocked when Jesus interacted with sinners, who were perceived as enemies. Because the apostles did not fully understand God's love, it was impossible for them to know the extent of its demands. They simply could not comprehend a mystical communion that united all people through grace and personal faith.

There can be no unity if we do not have the change of heart that comes from internalizing the love of Jesus Christ. God's love is the essence of true humanity and the unifying force in all relationships. Those deficient in agape love destroy the Christian witness and the potential it brings. A congregation unified in love can be a strong outreach in the prison setting.

The Priesthood as a Mystical Body

Dietrich Bonhoeffer developed the notion of the church as an interpersonal community that is defined by the complete self-forgetfulness of love (Dulles 1974, 48–49). This description reveals that the church is a fellowship with both God and other humans, where a person's community relationships depend on his or her spiritual life. The priesthood is signified and engendered by an external communion of faith, discipline, and the sacramental life.

The Spirit residing in each believer enables the world to experience the Creator. Although God is certainly present outside the church, the Spirit's presence within the priesthood draws people to Christ and unites them into one body. Without this "mystical presence," the collective organism that we call the church cannot exist.

Although this truth is rudimentary, it has somehow become lost in the teachings of the church.

The church must regain an emphasis on the inner life if it is to reach lost and dying people, including the numerous men and women who fill prisons all over the world. Only through union with the Holy Spirit can the church truly become the Bride of Christ and share in his life and ministry. Like the church in Laodicea, without the indwelling Spirit we become lukewarm and useless to God and the world (Rv 3:14–22).

In the harsh world of prison, where human power and manipulation influence lives, prisoners need to know that all power and control must be relinquished to the Holy Spirit—not easy for offenders, especially when they feel threatened by their environment. But regardless of the obstacles, emphasis on the control of the Holy Spirit is necessary for both personal development and ministry to others.

The mystical communion is given life in our relationship to God through Jesus Christ, which extends to our relationships with others. The dual dimension of this communion is important, for it distinguishes the church from other institutions. Avery Dulles (1974, 57) reports that since Vatican II, some Catholic writers have turned to the sociological concept of community as the principle for church renewal. While sociology is important, the "mystical" must be emphasized. The church is different from other institutions because through the church the Spirit unites with humanity.

The mystical communion creates a oneness that gives us freedom from the oppression that separates many people: "There is no longer Jew or Greek, there is no longer slave or free, there is no longer male and female, for all of you are one in Christ Jesus" (Gal 3:28). This communion is an important point of theology for those who suffer from the diversity, prejudice, and mistrust that is found in penal institutions. It shows that there is a bond between all humans in spite of our differences and imperfections. We are part of the communion even if we do not understand it. In other words, through faith we are members of the church in spite of ourselves.

As the priesthood of God, the church intercedes for others, bearing witness before the world to the liberating representation of Christ. The life of the new creation can be manifested only as an undivided whole. All individuals together live in one Spirit through which they find their identity and discover their place in the history of God's kingdom. Their service in the kingdom gives them all equal rights and points them toward solidarity (Moltmann 1975, 301–2).

Susanne Johnson (1989, 44) reminds us that the term *God's realm* does not refer to a place, but rather a dynamic way of life made possible by the Spirit. Only through the inner Spirit will distinctions and differences lose their power, making all Christians one in mutual healing and servanthood. In the mystical communion God unites every Christian throughout the ages, extending beyond geography and time. This is a powerful image when we consider the diversities that divide the church. Wallace Alston points out that "communion among the saints can never be achieved by human effort or simply organizational skills; that it is a gift of God" (1984, 42).

The early church would not have survived diversity and environmental tensions without the inner Spirit, who provided love, unity, and power. Luke tells us that, regardless of their differences, members of the early church somehow had all things in common (Acts 2:42–47). "The fellowship of the Spirit does not obscure or obliterate, but instead affirms differences, except when they are used in oppressive and dehumanizing ways" (Alston 1984, 156).

The church is called to share our struggles and to bear our burdens, thus fulfilling the law of Christ (Gal 6:2). However, this is only possible when the church becomes a mystical communion, using the gifts of the Spirit to heal and build the body of Christ into maturity.

People who share similar circumstances tend to manifest a collective spirit of sensitivity and concern for one another. While true in prison, inmates also develop an independence from others that is rooted in mistrust and survival. The loneliness and struggles of an inmate's particular situation influence his or her response, and these inmates often resist becoming part of a sharing and trusting community. Only through a "mystical" indwelling can prisoners unite in a true fellowship of love and trust.

Through the work of the Holy Spirit a healing ministry can be realized. Such a fellowship creates acceptance and a sense of identity and belonging where our own wounds become ministerial tools to heal and nurture others. Personal suffering can be a source of ministry to other people, rather than a curse. The priesthood is a place where diversity is understood in the context of God's will and creativity. It is a resource rather than a detriment. Different experiences and special gifts are used for mutual support, growth, and the continuation of ministry. When the Holy Spirit motivates our relationships, ministry is "ongoing and consistent, being woven into the fabric of all that happens, rather than presented on sporadic occasions as a new program" (Johnson 1989, 122).

4

Moving toward Improvement

Renewed Sense of Mission

The time has come for shallow rhetoric to be replaced by strong initiative and concrete action. Otherwise, prison mission statements of inmate rehabilitation are worthless. Prisoners are fully aware of the hypocrisy in what the system professes to do and what actually gets done. This dichotomy is a continuing source of frustration and anger for inmates who seek avenues for personal improvement and advancement.

Changes in any correctional department are impossible without dedicated and focused leadership at the highest levels. Management positions should not be held by politicians, but by experts in the field of corrections who recognize that improvements are both crucial and possible.

While individual prisons may implement some changes, the entire system must be revamped. The first step is to change the philosophy of corrections. This change can only occur if we provide prison staff members with an education that confronts the prevailing negativity in prison and focuses on real issues. Staff members must change their attitudes and form new objectives.

Staff Training and Continuing Education

An obvious problem in our prisons is the lack of pertinent training for employees. Although preliminary training is required, the extent of the training is questionable. Regardless of the position, no person should be permitted to work in a penal institution without completing sufficient course hours in basic psychology and the social sciences. Also, it is important that any educational program be given within the framework of ethnic, social, and racial diversity. Without pertinent training, prison staff lack the sensitivity and skills that their position requires. Institutional staff members are charged with the care, custody, and control of individuals who are under tremendous stress, necessitating behavior that reflects understanding, tolerance, and wisdom. How staff members respond to a given situation undoubtedly influences the reactions of prisoners, which in turn affects institutional security and safety.

To improve overall awareness and skills, correctional employees must participate in continuing education. In addition to classes on security and safety matters, professionals should lead seminars on inmate belief systems and human relationships. This training would help provide the knowledge and sensitivity that is so important for prison staff. In particular, the inmate stressors presented in chapter 2 would be excellent subject matter for employee reflection and dialogue.

Every staff member has a responsibility to inmates, fellow employees, and society to perform their duties in the most professional manner possible. This responsibility requires them to remember that security, safety, and the rehabilitation of offenders are the key objectives of the penal system. But these goals can only be realized through a meaningful and progressive educational program that permits an in-depth understanding of the inmate's emotional world.

There cannot be a changed philosophy or renewed sense of mission in corrections until employees are adequately trained. A system in which prison officials sit in board rooms theorizing change, believing that they actually have accomplished something is ludicrous. The correctional system needs an organized education program that is pertinent, permanent, creative, and progressive in nature. We simply cannot risk granting responsibility to employees who lack the initiative, expertise, and proper attitude to interact with inmate communities. A vigorous education program will unquestionably advance the professionalism needed to improve the entire system.

Some people believe that only treatment personnel such as counselors, chaplains, and psychologists need interpersonal skills. But this is far from the truth. In reality, security personnel have the broadest, and often most intense, contacts with felons. These individuals work in the cell blocks and other areas where inmates travel and congregate. Because they must also enforce institutional regulations, the interchanges between security officers and prisoners are the most potentially explosive. It is imperative, therefore, that security employees receive continuing education in psychology and the social sciences.

Living Conditions

Poor living conditions say a lot about how our society and government view convicted felons. It conveys a message that offenders do not deserve the same treatment that we deem necessary for other members of society. Simply stated, inadequate living conditions are proof that our prison system still engages in punishment and revenge. Inmates have difficulty trusting a government that advocates rehabilitation and, yet, defends deplorable environmental conditions.

Prisoners have many concerns relating to living conditions, but their foremost complaint addresses overcrowding and insufficient living space. Often, two individuals are housed in a small cell in a high-density cell block. The stress resulting from large, overcrowded facilities increases the possibility of inmate conflict. By their numbers alone, these prisons are more difficult to control and have a higher potential for open expressions of discontent and major disturbances. These factors should obviously be considered when designing new institutions. New correctional facilities should be built on a smaller scale, with increased living space and recreation areas and reduced cell blocks.

Smaller prisons are more personal, promoting positive attitudes for both inmates and staff. Also, many offenders believe that smaller facilities give them more identity, which enhances their self-esteem and sense of worth. While all prisons are unpredictable places regardless of their size, smaller institutions seem to create a more positive and stable environment. From a security viewpoint, they enable officers and other staff to know the residents better and have more control in an emergency.

In large, crowded penal communities prisoners experience stress as they compete for positions in educational and training programs.

There are also waiting lists to enter therapeutic groups, some of which are necessary for parole. The resulting stress sometimes produces expressions of anger toward peers and prison staff.

Prisons that take significant steps to improve their living conditions promote positive attitudes among inmates, which can affect productivity and tension levels. When offenders see improvements taking place, regardless how small, they feel that the system has some level of sensitivity and caring.

Many institutional changes would involve little cost to government, such as cosmetic work to improve the appearance of an institution. These projects would improve the environment, bring a sense of pride and ownership to inmate participation, and decrease idleness. Thousands of men and women call prison their home, and as a humane society we must find ways to improve these people-owned facilities. Any effort will undoubtedly be to our benefit.

Prison Activities

Inmate idleness is destructive and potentially dangerous. Lack of activity produces depression, anxiety, and a sense of worthlessness. As in any environment, idle people allow their imagination and emotions to form their attitudes and control their behavior, and in prison this can be disastrous for both inmates and institutions.

In the prison setting, activities help relieve tension, develop friendships, and create a social atmosphere. In some instances they build trust between residents. I have even seen activities improve the relationships between inmates and staff, particularly when common interests are involved. But regardless how one perceives their value, activities produce stability in a stressful community. A busy and productive prison is essential in order to improve attitudes.

Prisoners need a reason for living. Providing a positive atmosphere unquestionably affects their rehabilitation. Therefore, felons must experience the benefits of accomplishments, along with the hope that comes from establishing realistic goals. All of these proposals require institutional opportunities and encouragement. When either one is absent, prisons are simply places of stagnation and punishment.

Prison activities encompass a wide variety of experiences, including sports and educational programs. Depending on the circumstances, these activities are supervised by prison staff, contract professionals, or qualified volunteers. Each institution should assess their facility to ascertain the activities that will both benefit their population and meet security requirements. Many administrators resist allowing activities primarily because they fear that the change will bring security risks. But while security and safety can never be compromised in prison, it does not mean that activities are impossible.

Incentives

Most of what we accomplish in life brings some type of reward. Even in our Christian journey we are motivated by God's promise of a changed life. Although feeling good about ourselves is an important compensation, most people seek concrete benefits for their efforts, such as employment or financial gain. In many ways, it is this expectation that keeps us moving in a positive direction. Regardless of our circumstances, we progress through life impelled by rewards.

Lack of incentives in prison is a major reason for inmate negativity. When convicted felons discover that their personal advancements are not rewarded, they respond with an anger that, over time, turns to indifference. Incentives affect attitudes and behavior because they provide offenders with purpose and goals. Institutions that reward inmates for their accomplishments have more individuals who are engaged in positive endeavors.

Prisoners should not be promised anything that cannot be done. Residents are frequently told by counselors that progress in certain areas will guarantee them future privileges and possibly a changed status that will facilitate their parole. However, many of these promises do not materialize, which causes distress and anger in a prisoner who may have worked toward a specific goal for months. Decisions made by administrators at higher levels can change a felon's status and course of direction; therefore, prison employees should exercise caution. Staff promises are often the only hope that inmates have left.

Prisons can offer various types of incentives, including decreasing an inmate's sentence in return for good behavior and program involvement. Such an incentive keeps inmates busy, increases their productivity and skills, improves their attitudes and behavior, and brings them hope. Families of prisoners are also encouraged by such programs. They support inmates in their efforts to improve. Rehabilitation becomes a collective family effort.

Incentive programs are not without problems, but their overall results benefit everyone. They give residents the initiative to enter rehabilitation programs and become involved in self-improvement ventures. In addition, because a large number of peers share the same goals, mutual support becomes a reality.

Therapeutic Programs

All incarcerated felons are confronted with unjust prison conditions, legal abuse, and broken relationships. But therapeutic programs that focus on stress, personal loss, and unresolved anger are seldom available to them. Counseling sessions that examine these subjects would be helpful for all inmates, many of whom have never expressed their feelings in a therapeutic environment. This type of program would provide mutual support and a safe place for self-expression. Ventilation and feedback relieves tension and facilitates healing. Individual counseling and group sessions can also help eliminate some of the communication barriers unique to inmates.

Institutional adjustments and personal development are not possible unless offenders work through their unresolved stress and anger. However, it is impossible for them to do so without encouragement and professional assistance. As such, the correctional system must recognize the basic needs of prisoners and examine ways to implement therapeutic programs.

Treatment programs for sex offenders, individuals with aggressive behavior, alcoholics, and drug addicts are extremely important. Rehabilitation is difficult for individuals who are controlled by distorted beliefs and damaged emotions. Without help the situation only becomes worse. The cost of expanding therapeutic resources in prison is minimal when we consider the results of unprocessed loss, unrelenting stress, and repressed anger.

The Parole Process

Nothing is more important to the incarcerated than completing the steps necessary for parole. As inmates approach their minimum sentence date, they become increasingly concerned about the conditions that will permit their release. Meeting parole requirements is an arduous process that entails obtaining both an approved residence and established employment. Before reentering society, felons are required to have these two foundations in place.

For some inmates, obtaining a residence and employment is difficult and demands extensive networking over a long period of time.

Individuals can expend tremendous energy making telephone calls and writing letters, only to be continuously turned down. Often, family members and close friends do not trust the offender enough to help, especially if the felon is a habitual criminal. In some situations, prisoners have lost parole because of broken promises over residency or employment.

Moreover, inmates preparing for parole depend on prison staff for assistance. Networking and obtaining timely responses is difficult from inside a prison. Nevertheless, the extensive duties and large caseloads of institutional parole representatives and counselors make it impossible for prisoners to receive adequate help. For instance, in large correctional facilities it is not unusual for counselors to have caseloads that exceed one hundred and fifty inmates.

Since the incarcerated place all of their energy and hope in being released when their minimum time has been served, they need more understanding and support than is ordinarily available. In some cases, lack of assistance from staff members causes unnecessary anxiety that leads to aggressive behavior. A prisoner once said to me, "Can you imagine waiting years for your freedom, only to lose it because people who are supposed to help you simply don't care?" This individual was unable to make a telephone call needed to rectify a last minute problem that developed with his parole plan.

The first step in resolving parole problems is obviously to develop sensitivity toward inmates. Specific staff members should work as parole assistants, performing the duties that are beyond the time restraints of counselors and institutional parole representatives. Such a procedure would provide a much-needed service for anxiety-filled inmates who have been recommended for parole.

Prison Staff

Imprisoned criminals must learn to respect institutional authority. Obedience is part of their rehabilitation, and it is needed for the safe operation of a prison. But the apathy of some employees makes it impossible. Employees must firmly enforce regulations, but they can do so without prejudice and antagonism. Staff members who intentionally agitate and degrade inmates not only manifest unprofessionalism and ignorance but also jeopardize the lives of other people.

Custody employees who are assigned to cell blocks and spend a considerable amount of time with offenders can have a positive influence on them. This influence, however, requires discipline and an understanding of inmate tensions. Employees must constantly consider the repercussions of their actions. Understanding the dynamics of prison relationships comes from proper training and continuing education.

In order to diminish the military image of prison staff and simultaneously provide inmates with easier access to institutional services, some prisons utilize nonuniform management personnel in the housing units. This policy helps to break the communication barriers between felons and security employees. Nonuniform personnel reduce tensions by projecting supervisors as helpers rather than enforcement officers.

Community Volunteers

Many penal institutions permit a certain number of volunteers to enter the facility to engage in approved activities with inmates. These activities include sports, music programs, religious functions, and therapeutic programs. Some of these volunteers have been faithfully involved in prison work for years and have established trust in a particular institution.

Those who share their time and skills with inmates offer a unique and much-appreciated service. In fact, their presence may be the only contact some felons have with members of society. Volunteers build a bridge to the outside world, providing prisoners with a sense of being connected with the free community. This factor is extremely important to inmates who have little or no contact with the outside world. In many ways, volunteers serve as a lifeline to the freedom that inmates once took for granted.

Although institutional rules govern the relationships between prisoners and volunteers, they do not prevent offenders from developing emotional bonds. Some penal residents derive much of their self-worth and sense of direction from these guests. Prison volunteers provide a nonjudgmental, supportive, and caring presence; therefore, they help fill a deep void in the prisoner's life. Their presence affirms that there are people who care about the struggles and needs of convicted criminals and thus communicates the message that all human life has value.

Volunteers provide many services within the prison. They are teachers and living examples of social values and ethics. Their caring interaction shows inmates the importance of a giving relationship, of compromise, and of teamwork. In addition, they minister to loneliness and rejection. Their encouragement and acceptance gives offenders a feeling of self-worth and confidence that stimulates personal development.

Prison volunteers bring life and hope to people who desperately need acceptance and the motivation to improve their lives. They combat the fatalism of prison environments. In a sense, volunteers also help renew prison staff, enabling them to focus on the larger mission of the penal system—rehabilitation.

Special-Needs Inmates

All inmates have special needs, but two groups that stand out are those who need medical attention and those with life sentences. Offenders in these categories are confronted with situations that exacerbate the stress common to imprisonment. Accordingly, prison administrators need to examine the special needs of these individuals in an effort to improve their living conditions.

Prisoners with life sentences experience tensions that are unique to their circumstances. Looking through the iron bars of a cell and realizing what the future holds is traumatizing in a way that only other "lifers" understand. But these offenders must somehow find a way to work through their permanent loss of freedom.

Inmates who are given life sentences are extremely concerned about their environment—much more than prisoners who anticipate being released. When inmates realize that prison will be their final residence, they become increasingly sensitive to their surroundings. For example, they undergo considerable stress when other residents leave the institution for community programs, furloughs, or parole. Seeing others experience freedom is a constant source of anguish for those who have lost all hope of returning to society.

Prisoners with long sentences are more at ease living with peers who are in the same situation. Such conditions lessen the anxiety of continuously seeing other residents released and develops social bonding and support systems for individuals who more readily identify with one another.

All prisoners have difficulty with change, especially those facing life sentences. The most difficult changes for these inmates involve their cell partners. When inmates with life sentences are placed in the general population, they are subject to numerous cell changes during their incarceration. These changes mean adjusting to a new living companion, and the mere anticipation of more change brings unrelenting anxiety and tension. When there cannot be separate prisons for inmates with life sentences, they should be given single cells in their own housing unit.

Lifers also need programs that confront idleness, improve self-worth, and contribute to development. We tend to view these inmates as being outside the scope of rehabilitation efforts, which affects the educational and training opportunities that are available to them. Many programs in correctional facilities, particularly the most worthwhile, are used as vehicles to prepare offenders for their return to society. Because the majority of lifers will not return to society, they are not priority candidates for academic and job skills training.

While it is logical to give opportunities for education and job training to inmates who will return to society, a growing number of felons with life sentences desperately need to be engaged in self-improvement activities also. Education and training improves the quality of life for prisoners. Inmates who engage in self-improvement activities not only help themselves but also are more likely to assist their peers.

Prisoners with life sentences must find a reason to continue living and maintaining positive attitudes and acceptable behavior—not an easy task for people who know that prison is their only future. It is wrong to believe that these residents do not require stimulation simply because they will not return to society. Lifers have intense struggles with identity and self-worth. Without self-improvement programs the motivation for living is gone. They lose concern and respect for other people, which can be dangerous in prison. Without educational and other self-improvement programs their lives have little value and no direction.

Some men and women in prison have truly been rehabilitated, but because of legal inflexibility they remain prisoners for life. A number of these offenders may have committed their crimes as teenagers under the strong influence of peers, or even adult criminals. Some of them have even exceeded the criteria that is required of other inmates for parole, but unless they receive a pardon from the governor they will never be released. Some inmates can spend more than twenty years in a correctional facility with an impeccable institutional record. They can prove themselves to be remorseful, nonviolent, and productive. Yet, because of their sentence they will die in prison, even though they have shown every sign of being rehabilitated.

I do not mean to suggest that everyone serving a life sentence should be considered for early release. Many of these prisoners do not change, and consequently they cannot be released from prison. It is affirming, however, to know that there are lifers who have been rehabilitated and are no longer a threat to society. Some of these inmates are not career criminals or incurable deviants, and after serving a long prison sentence they deserve to live the remainder of their lives as free individuals.

Inmates with medical problems also have special needs. Residents with chronic medical conditions or terminal illnesses require specialized care. Whether they have cancer, AIDS, or kidney failure, these inmates usually need continuous care in a comfortable environment. Some medical cases also call for frequent visits to community hospitals. But even when prisons have adequate treatment facilities, the quality of care is sometimes questionable.

The most troubling reality for inmates who are ill is their environment. When seriously ill residents are forced to live in the general population, one questions the wisdom and intent of administrators. Placing recovering, chronically ill, and terminal inmates in cells with other prisoners in overcrowded housing units borders on inhumane treatment. The noise, discomfort, relational friction, inadequate attention, and potential danger in these cell blocks only exacerbates medical conditions. Although some ill prisoners desire to live among the general population, they should not dictate medical decisions.

Part of the solution to inadequate medical treatment is to construct prison hospitals that are designed to treat prisoners in certain geographical areas. Depending on the circumstances, these hospitals could be involved in both short-term and extended care. They should be located near major community hospitals that are equipped to respond to any emergency. They would be more efficient, provide better treatment, reduce medical and operational costs, lessen inmate and family tensions, and hopefully address some of the lawsuits that are filed against the correctional system for inadequate medical care. When we view the increasing number of prison medical cases in light of existing capabilities, the investment involved in building prison hospitals is certainly worth considering.

Family Deaths

The deepest losses for inmates are family deaths, for they create feelings of intense guilt and helplessness. Often, their anxiety manifests itself in depression and anger. Seldom are there therapeutic resources available to help them process their feelings. If not for support from peers, inmates would go through the grieving process alone.

Stress related to family deaths increases when residents are unable to attend funerals. The most common reason for this is lack of finances. Prisoners are transported to funerals by law enforcement agencies, such as county sheriffs, and the fees are often too high for inmates and their families. I have counseled many offenders who were unable to be present at a loved one's funeral for financial reasons. Needless to say, the wounds that result from being unable to say goodbye are painful. It is common for prisoners with long sentences to experience multiple family deaths while they are incarcerated. In many cases, these inmates are unable to attend any of the funerals.

An inmate's ability to attend family funerals must be addressed by prison officials. Prisons should network with other law enforcement agencies to help provide supervised forms of transportation. Moreover, an inmate organization may even consider assuming part of the cost of transportation. The inability to grieve for loved ones is not a minor irritant for felons, but rather an ongoing cause for tension and negative attitudes.

Prison Sentences

Depending on the state, county, and judge involved in a criminal case, the sentences given to offenders for the same classification of crime vary. This situation is understandable in that the courts must consider the past record of a convicted criminal and the circumstances of the offense. We must provide the courts with such latitude. Yet, while there are substantial grounds for varying sentences, flexibility does have its share of problems and injustices.

Many factors contribute to the length of an individual's prison sentence, and it is the court's responsibility to weigh all the data before making a reasonable decision. However, not only are the courts given too much leeway, but sometimes external elements influence the decision making—for example, the political mood at the time of the trial. Two separate cases for second-degree murder may have the same set of circumstances, both being committed out of passion by first time offenders; but the prison sentences for these felons can be vastly different. When we reflect on the value of freedom, this situation raises questions about our judicial system and its claim of equal justice.

Unfortunately, sentencing decisions involve more than societal concerns and legal reasoning. They are also influenced by political aspirations, the personalities and beliefs of individual judges, the influences of attorneys and victims, and the financial and intellectual abilities of defendants. These elements strongly determine the length of prison sentences, and the results can be devastating.

Our sentencing structure needs to be changed to reflect uniformity and fairness for all offenders. As inmates interact with one another they quickly become aware of the disparity between their prison sentences. Such disparity reinforces their view of a judicial system in which equality and equal justice are nonexistent.

Aftercare

A critical time for convicted felons is when they leave prison and return to the community. The move from institutional life to society is difficult for many reasons. Inmates initially respond to freedom with expectant joy and excitement, but these feelings begin to fade when they are confronted with new economic realities.

Released inmates must also face influences and temptations that did not exist in prison. Incarceration is an isolated and structured life that is carefully supervised by prison staff. With freedom, however, released felons find new concerns. Some people lose their way and slip back into old habits, addictions, and a refusal or inability to accept responsibility. Moreover, most released inmates reside in high-crime areas where negative influences are the strongest.

Individuals who return to prison because of parole violations or new criminal charges often claim that economic struggles drove them to commit these acts. When people leave prison, they immediately realize that without credit they have no purchasing power. Their small incomes are simply not enough to purchase what they need, least of all the "luxury" items their family members and friends possess. In addition, inmates who lack marketable skills and education find employment opportunities sparse and wages menial. Many employers find it hard to trust those who have committed serious crimes, which adds to employment difficulties. The insecurity and hostility these conditions create leads many felons back to the criminal world of quick money.

There is nothing more important for released prisoners than aftercare—after all, these individuals seldom have the resources to become stable citizens on their own. They need assistance that begins while they are still incarcerated. In other words, networking prior to release is necessary to prevent inmates from being overwhelmed by the new challenges of freedom, whether they receive support from a local church, a counseling agency, a therapeutic center, a workshop, or a job training program. Many individuals and organizations can assist returning felons but only through community awareness and inmate networking.

At the recommendation of prison administrators, some inmates receive an early review and are released to approved community centers. These centers are excellent transitional facilities because they enable released felons to progressively move through the adjustments of discovery and responsibility before assuming residency in a local community. But they are few in number; therefore, not all qualified candidates are allowed into the program. Moreover, many inmates need additional assistance.

Some advocates of punishment believe that offenders should struggle on their own. Such an attitude only leads individuals back to prison and creates added burdens for the correctional system. It stands to reason that if relatively stable people require encouragement and support, then liberated inmates certainly have the same needs.

The development of societal support systems for prisoners is a realistic goal, but community awareness is necessary. We cannot submit to the negative attitudes and fatalism of those who view convicted criminals as hopeless causes. Instead, we must find ways to communicate the needs of inmates and their families to others. Communities can make a difference in the life of a released prisoner. Like the many volunteers who visit our prisons, there are people in every community who believe that a compassionate outreach from society will help offenders turn their lives around.

Relationships influence success; therefore, in addition to structured support, released offenders need to have positive friendships that will help them resist any circumstances that are detrimental to their welfare. In their weakened and susceptible state, even brief encounters with the wrong people could lead released felons back to prison.

Church groups are increasingly becoming involved in outreach programs to prisoners and their families, and they have been a stabilizing force. Members of these groups are often instrumental in keeping felons engaged in constructive relationships and productive activities.

Crime and incarceration affect families, society, and the legal system. Such being the case, our goal should be collective involvement through awareness. An effective way to have a positive impact is to share our knowledge with others. For example, when experts from the field of corrections speak at spiritual gatherings and community events, they lay the groundwork for aftercare.

The Church

Prison ministry brings encouragement and hope to men and women who seek a new direction. While imprisonment is an extreme hardship, it forces residents to reflect on the past and ponder the future. At this point the church frequently comes into focus. Many prisoners have Christian roots, and during their darkest hours these roots are remembered. Prison life leads individuals to look to the spiritual realm for solutions to their problems. They come to know the claims and promises of Jesus Christ and his church.

Personal guilt and an adverse environment make spiritual advancements difficult. Within the church, however, solutions to various problems do exist. Not only can inmates find relief from their agonizing guilt, but they discover that Christ promises to provide the sustaining grace they desperately need. The church offers the grace of encouragement and support and a feeling of self-worth and belonging. As a result, personal transformation and an outreach to others begins in prison.

Regardless how we perceive prison ministry or the validity of inmate responses to religion, the church serves as a continuing source of grace and hope for those who truly desire to change their lives. Even when prisoners refuse to respond to the gospel, the church remains a positive influence and call to every sinner because it offers forgiveness and a new life in Jesus Christ.

Conclusion

Many stereotypes surround the incarcerated. Although *Ministry to the Incarcerated* has not specifically addressed this issue, it has hopefully provided some understanding of inmate attitudes and behavior.

Crime can never be justified, nor can the prison system be abolished. But every effort must be made to improve penal conditions and the rehabilitation process. Changing the correctional system requires a desire to do so, strong leadership, expertise, and concrete action at upper management levels. However, the responsibility extends to all prison staff because, in one way or another, every employee influences inmates. The church is certainly instrumental in this change; thus, it is essential that ministry exemplify Christ by addressing needs and issues with sensitivity, wisdom, and compassion.

Mistrust makes it difficult for offenders to grow in faith and love. Furthermore, inmates often view religious commitment with suspicion or see it as a weakness. For this reason, the results of many Christian efforts are short-lived.

Unlike other settings, the tensions, unpredictability, and extreme conditions found in prison do not fade over time. Therefore, when evaluating methods of pastoral care and evangelistic outreach, the church must understand the unique obstacles to spiritual development in prison and seek paradigms and other educational tools that will provide the most effective ministry.

This book is a realistic evaluation of an inmate's difficulties in spiritual development. But it also looks toward a future when many of these obstacles will be overcome through institutional improvements and the continuous application of the gospel. The goal of the church is for all to be free in Christ, including the incarcerated and those trapped in the prisons created in the human spirit by sin. Jesus came so that we might have life, and have it abundantly. The church cannot force personal change, but it can be a viable channel of transforming and sustaining grace for those who seek a new life.

Afterword

On May 2, 1995, I was the chaplain for Pennsylvania's first execution since 1962, which was held at the State Correctional Institution at Rockview. The inmate was Keith Zettlemoyer, age thirty-nine, who was convicted in the shooting death of a friend who planned to testify against him in a robbery trial. After fourteen years as a death row inmate, Zettlemoyer decided to terminate any efforts at delaying or overturning his death sentence. He voiced these sentiments to individuals and agencies, indicating that he desired to end his earthly bondage.

On the above date I spent seven hours with Zettlemoyer. Our conversation, although it was broad, primarily focused on spiritual matters. In addition to these discussions, I administered the Eucharist and prayed with him on three occasions. At approximately 9:45 P.M. he was removed from his cell, strapped onto a gurney, and taken to the adjoining execution chamber where security personnel and technicians prepared him for lethal injection. I was permitted to accompany him during this transitional stage.

Prior to meeting Zettlemoyer I read some background information about his personality and criminal case. I also prayed for wisdom and guidance. Rather than approach him with a planned agenda, my intention was merely to listen, allowing him to take the lead. My desire was to be a pastor in whatever way possible.

Although he lacked formal education, I found Keith Zettlemoyer to be articulate and in command of the English language. He communicated his beliefs and feelings with both sensitivity and skill. He also manifested concern toward others, including those charged with his custody and care. On several occasions he verbally communicated a caring attitude toward the execution team. His entire demeanor was one of inner peace and gentleness.

Zettlemoyer shared information about his parents and four sisters. As we spoke he revealed deep regret for his past life and how it affected family relationships. His most painful expression related to his parents. He shared his burdens concerning their grief over his incarceration and imminent death. As he mentioned each family member by name there were expressions of both love and sorrow. In this sharing he often remembered pleasurable family situations.

I cannot emphasize enough the remorse that Zettlemoyer communicated. Throughout our time together he often digressed from a particular subject to reiterate the horror of his crime. These were intense moments in which he relived the killing with detail. He informed me that his crime had tortured him during his imprisonment, especially since he had become a Christian about twelve years ago. One area of guilt pertained to the victim's spiritual state at his time of death. Zettlemoyer could not rid himself of the belief that his victim possibly died without salvation. We addressed this issue in our dialogue.

Zettlemoyer spoke warmly about the victim's mother, who openly voiced her opinion against capital punishment. He was simply astounded that she sought to block his execution. Her concern brought him a sense of comfort and peace as he contemplated his own death.

Spiritual Insights

Keith Zettlemoyer died for the crime of murder, but he left this life as a Christian who experienced through the witness of the Spirit the forgiveness of God. He was saved. He wanted me to know that although he was somewhat anxious about his execution, his faith was strong.

During my seven hour visit with Zettlemoyer some of my beliefs concerning prison ministry were reinforced. His changed life clearly indicated to me that through the power of Christ people can change. The following is a brief sketch reflecting the insights of an inmate who was on death row for fourteen years. It represents the thoughts of a man who relentlessly prayed and studied Scripture and who pondered even the smallest of spiritual issues.

Christian Fellowship

Keith Zettlemoyer asked me this question: Can you imagine experiencing spiritual rebirth through Jesus Christ and never being able to share your joy with other people? In other words, how would it feel to become a living part of the body of Christ and not be able to worship and experience fellowship with other believers? According to Zettlemoyer, this is exactly how he lived since he was incarcerated in a maximum security cell block.

Death row inmates find themselves removed from the spiritual nurturing that is so desperately needed in their lives. Such was the case with Keith Zettlemoyer. Not providing these individuals with spiritual opportunities is to deny their needs.

On the eve of his execution Zettlemoyer informed me that I would be his Christian fellowship, emphasizing that Christ is present where two or three are gathered in his name. His sole focus during these last hours was to spend his time with another Christian with whom he could pray and share his concerns.

Can you imagine being a Christian living in total isolation? This death row inmate taught me the importance of the local church with its many dimensions of grace. He dreamed of being around other Christians who share the same hopes. Over the years Zettlemoyer pondered many theological questions without a pastor to discuss them with. His message was clear: the church is a gift that so many people take for granted and abuse. As such, the sustaining and nurturing grace of God is lost.

The Ministry of Presence

There are simply no words to express the importance of my presence to Keith Zettlemoyer. I was his pastor, source of fellowship and support, and prayer partner. Throughout it all was the representation of Christ and his church. He wanted me there, and his desire was to communicate his deepest feelings with someone who possessed the same spirit.

Nothing was more important to Zettlemoyer than the church being there for him. Every second was crucial. On several occasions he asked me for the time, after which he would lead me into another area of spirituality. As the minutes ticked away, he wanted to be certain that my presence would meet his perceived needs.

I approached Zettlemoyer with certain pastoral thoughts, but I had no specific plan. Instead, I allowed the Spirit to guide the ministry. Little did I know just how important my presence would be and how many facets of ministry would take place.

I knew the importance of a caring presence, but I never viewed it from as many perspectives as I did that evening. I learned that presence involves listening more than speaking, caring more than knowledge.

The Eucharist—Theology of the Cross

Receiving the sacrament of Holy Communion was a blessing to Keith Zettlemoyer. When he realized that we were going to partake of this sacrament he became emotional. Zettlemoyer told me that Holy Communion brings him very close to the Lord. Through the Eucharist his own suffering gets swallowed up in the suffering of Jesus Christ.

Keith saw the Eucharist as a time of special sacredness in which Christ was present in a real way. Communion was also his assurance of God's forgiveness for a crime that people cannot forgive. As he received the elements he repeated the sentences of institution, with each word having profound significance for him.

The Priesthood of Servants

A continuing source of agony for Zettlemoyer was his inability to serve God in what he considered to be concrete ways. Most of his contacts were with prison staff. Therefore, his only hope was that he was a witness to them. He truly wanted to believe that he was doing God's will, but being removed from the general population made it impossible for him to touch the lives of others. Even though he knew that he was not saved by works, he wanted the blessing of being able to serve God in a community setting.

We too often understand Christian service as a burden rather than a blessing. Instead of sharing what God has given us, we try to keep our lives for ourselves. It is no wonder that we lack much of the peace and joy that God makes available to us.

Faith

Zettlemoyer spoke about faith in God with deep emotion, believing that it was only grace that led him to Jesus Christ. He also knew that it was only grace and faith that sustained him through his many years of isolation, even enabling him to grow spiritually in his death row environment.

On death row there is no one to lean on for understanding, strength, and encouragement. This separation leads many inmates to despair and emotional distress. Zettlemoyer had his bouts with depression, but through it all he maintained his faith in Christ. His faith is what gave him peace when he stretched out his arms to receive the lethal injection.

So many people claim to have faith, but there remains a strong dependence on the world. This dependence prevents individuals from developing a trust that will carry them through difficult trials. Faith enables people to grow and serve God in the midst of life's trials. In prison one cannot rely on the world. As Zettlemoyer emphatically stated, on death row there is only God.

Forgiveness

Zettlemoyer could not explain how God could forgive him for such an atrocious crime, but he nonetheless claimed an inner witness of assurance. He saw God's forgiveness as a mystery that could not be explained—only experienced. He knew that people did not forgive him, but he understood and maintained a humble spirit toward all people, knowing how crime affects our lives.

Zettlemoyer had questions about sins of omission. He believed that with the grace of forgiveness came the responsibility to serve God by reaching out to others. Again he expressed his concern, for being on death row seemed to make serving others impossible.

Final Thoughts

The statement that "God works in mysterious ways" is one that is now etched in my mind. How could I ever have imagined that a man convicted of murder would be such a strong witness on the day of his execution. Just before his death Keith Zettlemoyer inquired, What will you say to people who ask you about this execution? I was shocked by the question and unable to respond adequately, telling him that the thought had not crossed my mind.

Nevertheless, I felt compelled to write this sketch. In fact, the book would have been incomplete without it.

My interaction with Keith Zettlemoyer is certainly a witness of God's forgiveness. It is also a penetrating example of the peace and assurance that accompanies forgiveness. What will I tell people about this execution? I will tell them the truth. Keith Zettlemoyer died with the peace of God in his heart. He told me that his only problem with the death penalty related to the unsaved—those who are executed without Jesus Christ in their hearts.

What I have written does not diminish Zettlemoyer's guilt for the crime he committed, nor is it intended to paint him as someone who has attained a certain level of spirituality. It is, however, an accurate account of his thoughts and faith during the last hours of his life. In a very real sense, it is a witness of this man's changed life, a witness that he desperately wanted to communicate. Hopefully, it will somehow be a continuing witness of the power of Jesus Christ.

Appendix
Curriculum Outlines

The nurturing function of the church includes education, with the uniqueness of the congregation and the particular environment being important factors. While prisoners have many needs, certain areas should be prioritized. Inmates share many of the same struggles, among which are stress, anger, and relational division. If these ideas are not adequately communicated, spiritual development is stifled. Therefore, in-depth study and dialogue are needed on these subjects.

The curriculum outlines that follow provide substantial material for study and discussion on the obstacles to prison ministry. Although particular Scripture passages may be debated in terms of hermeneutics, each can apply in some way. It is at the discretion of the teacher to either employ or discard biblical references or portions of an outline.

Stress

This outline is designed to provide an understanding of the many causes for stress in order to improve coping mechanisms, facilitate changes, and stimulate emotional and spiritual growth. By using this study on stress, we can

1. develop the ability to recognize damaging areas of stress in a person's life;
2. examine the processes through which individuals bring stress into their lives;
3. comprehend how tensions are interrelated and how they affect all facets of life;
4. develop the ability to accept realities that cannot be changed;
5. provide the initiative and direction to restructure areas where change is necessary;
6. learn to use preventive measures, resources, and practical applications to alleviate tension; and
7. remove stress-related obstacles that block emotional maturity, sanctification, and relational unity.

I. Definition
   A. Mentally or emotionally disruptive or disquieting influence
   B. Some manner of distress
   C. Response to excessive demands
   D. Response relating to guilt and/or sin (Gn 42:21; Lam 1:18–20)
II. Causes
   A. Life situations
      1. Health (Jb 7:5, 11, 15, 16)
      2. Socioeconomic standing
      3. Relational strife
      4. Spiritual desolation (Mi 6:13)
      5. Circumstances (Gn 32:6–7)
      6. Employment
      7. Incarceration (2 Tm 2:9)
   B. Repression and suppression (Jas 5:16)
      1. Unconscious or conscious exclusion of painful impulses
         a) Buried emotions
      2. Need for proper ventilation (Eph 4:26–27)
         a) Painful process
         b) Requires discipline, honesty, and energy (Heb 2:11)
   C. Depression (Jb 3)
      1. Anger turned inward (1 Kgs 21:1–4)
         a) Physical and emotional results (Prv 13:12)
         b) Causes (Jon 4:1–4)
   D. Poor self-concept
      1. Produced by others, self, or situation (Ex 4:10; Jer 1:6; 1 Cor 15:9)
         a) Poor health
         b) Physical appearance
         c) Financial problems
         d) Perceived failures and/or mistakes
         e) Lack of accomplishments
         f) Life-cycle or other transitions
         g) Other personal factors
   E. Personal threats
      1. Self-esteem, ego, well being (1 Sm 18:6–8; Est 3:2–6)
      2. Safety (1 Sm 21:10–15; 30:6)

   3. Reputation (1 Sm 15:1–31)

   4. Separation and loss

F. Personal expectations (Lk 10:38–42)

   1. Unrealistic goals

   2. Inappropriate desires

   3. Perfectionism

   4. Excessive involvement in some activity

   5. Competition, drive for success

   6. Distorted perspectives

   7. Wrong priorities

   8. Many responsibilities

G. Improper responses

   1. Authority (Rom 13:1; Ti 3:1; 1 Pt 2:13–14)

   2. Adversity (Eccl 7:14)

   3. Relationships (Jn 15:13)

   4. Blocked desires or goals

   5. Rejections

   6. Societal or world events

H. Financial difficulties

   1. Overextended (Prv 22:7)

   2. Inadequate income (1 Kgs 17:12)

   3. Wrong focus (Eccl 2:20)

   4. Distorted philosophy (Eccl 5:12)

I. Unproductive life

   1. Idleness

   2. Lack of accomplishments

   3. No direction, void of purpose

   4. Inferiority and insecurity

J. Unmet needs (Mt 6:25–34; Phil 4:6)

   1. Conscious or unconscious

   2. Imagined or real

K. Materialism (Mt 19:16–22)

   1. Real needs undermined by the world

   2. Attempt to fill void

     a) Search for self-worth, purpose, power, recognition

   3. Produces more difficulties

     a) Dissatisfaction from false answers

     b) Emotional and spiritual struggles

L. Guilt
  1. False or unproductive life
  2. Spiritual conviction (Ps 51)
  3. Family responsibilities
  4. Mistakes and failures (Mt 27:3–5; Lk 22:54–62)
  5. Lost opportunities
  6. Crime and incarceration
  7. Embarrassment/shame (Gn 3:9–10; Ezr 9:5–6)

M. Loss
  1. Free will and control of one's life
  2. Dignity and respect
  3. Support systems—family, friends, other (Jb 19:19)
  4. Social and other important events
  5. Trust of others (Lk 22:39–48)
  6. Opportunities
  7. Divorce, death, separation
  8. Socialization
  9. Finances

N. Peer pressure (Gal 2:11–14)
  1. To conform to individuals, groups, or institutions
  2. Personal threats—overt or latent
  3. Criticism or judgment
  4. Rejection and isolation
  5. Projected guilt

O. Family difficulties
  1. Marital problems
  2. Extended family, in-laws
  3. Children

P. Appearance and diet
  1. Negative social reactions
  2. Poor self-image, embarrassment
  3. Personal guilt
  4. Sense of failure and loss of control
  5. Lost opportunities
  6. Impact on relationships
    Note: Dieting can increase certain forms of stress.

Q. Health problems
  1. Acceptance is difficult
  2. Support is important
  3. Spiritual life essential (2 Kgs 20:1–2)
  4. Worry affects emotions

R. Unrighteous living (Rom 6:12, 23)
1. Influence on every aspect of life (1 Cor 5:6–7)
    a) Present and future
2. Compromise of biblical truths (Jas 2:10)
3. Neglected priorities
4. Wrong focus

III. Treatment
    A. Recognition
    1. Identification and honest assessment
    2. Desire for change (Rom 12:1–2; 13:14)
    3. Requires discipline and energy
    4. Practice prevention
    B. Understanding of life's realities
    1. Temptations (Jas 1:13–15)
    2. Changes and uncertainties
    3. Trials and losses
    4. Certain things cannot be changed (Mt 6:34)
    C. Restructure
    1. Intercept negative patterns
    2. Redirect energies
    3. Change in philosophy
    4. Environmental change
    5. Proper balance of time
    6. Occupational considerations
    7. Examination of involvement and goals
    8. Spiritual focus needed (Is 26:3; Mt 6:33;
       Eph 4:22–24)
    9. Realistic expectations
        a) Self, others, institutional, societal, relational,
        occupational
    10. Delegation of tasks
    D. Solitude and silence (Ps 4:4; 46:10)
    1. Place and/or inner state
        a) Beyond senses and distractions
        b) Requires discipline
    2. Brings personal awareness (Ps 39:3–4)
    3. Experience God's revelations (Jos 1:8; Ps 119:15–16,
       97–104)
    4. Allows an emptying of self (Ps 131:1–2)
    5. Opens the unconscious

      6. Eliminates nervous tension

      7. Reveals burdens and needs

      8. Realization of grace (Ps 63:5–8)

      9. Helps awaken praise and thanksgiving (Ps 104:33–34)

    10. Eliminates anger (Ps 4:4)

    11. Brings peace and restoration (Ps 23:2)

    12. Gives strength and confidence (Is 30:15)

    13. Tool for preparation, molding, and growth

    14. Results in renewal (Is 41:1)

E. Journaling (see Klug 1982, 9–129)

      1. Provides self-discovery—a mirror of the soul

        a) Record of beliefs, emotions, reactions, and observations

      2. Aids concentration

      3. Safety valve for emotions

        a) Safe means of expression

      4. Friend and confidant

      5. Tool for personal growth

        a) Allows in-depth examination

        b) Reflects needs, helps provide solutions

      6. Develops creativity

        a) Place and time to generate ideas

      7. Aids devotional life

        a) Spiritual reflection and scriptural meditation

      8. Creates discipline and concentration

        a) Needed for renewal and growth

      9. Helps maintain perspective

        a) A "thinking through" process

        b) Weigh alternatives

        c) Clarify beliefs

        d) Deeper penetration into ideas and experiences

    10. Setting and managing goals

        a) Keeps goals in the foreground

        b) Vision of movement

    11. Enables hindsight

        a) Clears the way for the future

    12. Clarify needs, values, and priorities

F. Ministry to self

      1. Activities, special interests

      2. Fellowship (Eccl 4:9–12; Gal 6:2; 1 Thes 5:11; Heb 10:24–25)

    3. Quality family time

    4. Solitude and rest (Mk 6:30–32)

    5. Experiencing God's creation

    6. Learning to laugh (Prv 17:22)

       a) Lightens burdens and intensity

       b) Promotes feelings of well-being

G. Stability and security

    1. Weigh results of change

       a) Personal and family effects

       b) Present and future

    2. Question unnecessary change

       a) Take time to make decisions (Prv 11:14)

       b) Consider everything

H. Change habits

    1. Physical—damaging to health (1 Cor 3:16–11; 6:19–20)

    2. Emotional—responses to situations (Prv 16:32; 25:28; Jas 1:19–20)

    3. Relational—ways of relating

I. Nurture positive relationships (Prv 17:17; 27:6)

    1. Brings personal growth (Prv 27:17)

    2. Provides support systems

    3. Avenues for safe ventilation

    4. Pleasurable fellowship (2 Sm 1:26; Ps 133:1)

    5. Broaden insights and philosophical views

J. Constructive and righteous living

    1. Brings peace and confidence (Is 32:17)

    2. Work is important (Prv 22:29; 1 Thes 5:14)

    3. Develop potentials (Prv 21:5)

    4. Accept responsibility (Gal 6:4–5)

    5. Achievement and service brings satisfaction

K. Service

    1. Removes attention from self (Phil 2:3)

    2. Produces positive feelings

       a) Self-worth, meaning, purpose (Mt 25:14–30)

    3. Examples of Christ (Mk 10:43–45; Phil 2:4–11)

    4. Brings blessings (Lk 6:38)

L. Realistic expectations (Ps 131:1; Jas 4:13–15)

    1. Self, family, and others

    2. Employment

    3. Institutions

    4. Society, life

M. Acceptance (Mt 6:34; Phil 4:19)
   1. Life's realities
   2. What cannot be changed
   3. Self and others
   4. Present situation

N. Learn contentment
   1. Inner peace—condition of the heart
     a) Spiritual reality
     b) Peace with self, God, others, and creation
       (Rom 12:18; 2 Cor 13:11; 1 Thes 5:13; Heb 12:14)
     c) Joy of being and experiencing (Neh 8:10)

O. Emotional distancing
   1. From certain people and situations
     a) For self-protection

P. Cognition
   1. Honest self-examination (2 Cor 13:5; Jas 5:16)
     a) Feelings and behavior (Gal 6:3–5)
   2. Activate reason and self-control (Prv 16:32; 25:28;
     2 Pt 1:5–7)
     a) Prevents emotions from taking control
   3. Weigh alternatives
     a) Awareness of possible consequences

Q. Sex
   1. Gift for married couples (1 Cor 7:1–7)
   2. Discipline required for singles (1 Cor 6:16–20; Heb 13:4)
   3. Result of immorality (Prv 5:20–23)

R. Knowledge of roles and boundaries
   1. Within family system (Eph 5:22–6:9; Col 3:18–25)
   2. Social and legal (Rom 13:1–10; 1 Pt 2:13–19)
   3. Spiritual (1 Tm 5:17; Heb 13:7)

S. Living in the present
   1. Not controlled by the past (Phil 3:13–14)
   2. Trusting God for future (Mt 6:25–34; Phil 4:6)
   3. Live with anticipation and hope (Heb 6:17–19)

T. Proper expression of anger (Eph 4:26–27)
   1. Elimination of hostility (Prv 15:1, 18)
   2. Discipline and control necessary (Prv 16:32; 25:28)

U. Exercise and fitness
   1. Noncompetitive
   2. Chemical reactions dispel stress

      3. Form of safe ventilation

      4. Improves self-esteem

      5. Has social dimensions

  V. Communications (Prv 27:9, 17)

      1. Visits, letters, telephone calls

        a) Support

        b) Relieves worry

 W. Counseling (Prv 11:14; 15:22; 19:20; 20:18; 27:9)

      1. Professional or nonprofessional

        a) Expression on feeling level

        b) Nonparticipant feedback

        c) Enables a "working through" process

IV. Spiritual life

  A. Reconciliation (Ps 34:14)

      1. With God, family, others, and authority

        a) Must seek forgiveness—God, others, and self

        b) Forgiving is a choice (Mt 18:21–35)

        c) Recognizing imperfections in self enables understanding of others (Mt 7:1–5)

  B. Understanding biblical contentment (Heb 13:5–6)

      1. Paul's words (Phil 4:11–13)

      2. Attitude of the heart—life of faith

      3. State of mind (Is 26:3)

  C. Positive thoughts (Phil 4:8; Col 3:1–2)

      1. Affect perception and responses

      2. Impact on others

  D. Repentance (1 Jn 1:9)

      1. A way of life (Ps 51:17)

      2. Removes guilt, brings renewal (1 Cor 15:31)

  E. Prayer

      1. Seek gifts of the Holy Spirit (1 Cor 12:31)

      2. All gifts relating to love (1 Cor 13; 14:12)

      3. Sensitivity to God (Ps 25:5; Is 55:6–9)

      4. Desire and ability to serve (Phil 2:3–8)

  F. Clear sense of purpose (2 Cor 4:18)

      1. Focus on eternal things (Mt 6:19–21)

  G. Fellowship with believers

      1. Mutual support (Gal 6:2; 1 Thes 5:11; Heb 10:24–25)

      2. Necessary for emotional and spiritual growth

      3. Healing community

    H. Service (Mk 10:42–45; 2 Cor 1:3–4; Gal 6:9–10; 1 Thes 5:15)
       1. Accountability to God (Mt 25:14–30)
    I. Giving thanks and praise (Ps 68:19; 100; 107:1–9)
       1. Emphasis on God's providence
       2. Reflection on divine care (Ps 31:19; 63:7)
       3. Positive thoughts bring peace and comfort
    J. Eucharist
       1. Emphasis on God's love
       2. Confession relieves guilt (1 Jn 1:9)
       3. Community fellowship is comforting
       4. Establishes hope
    K. Meditation on Scripture
       1. Christ's ministry
       2. Sustaining grace (Rom 8:28; 2 Cor 12:9–10; 1 Jn 4:4)

Anger

This study examines the causes of anger in the human developmental stages by focusing on past and present environmental influences. It should be used as a vehicle to

1. encourage the discovery of unresolved emotional issues, specifically those of a relational and institutional nature;
2. provide an understanding of the continuing destructive nature of improperly expressed anger;
3. examine anger in a spiritual context, emphasizing biblical warnings against unrighteous indignation;
4. develop therapeutic and spiritual techniques for processing and redirecting negative energies;
5. develop coping mechanisms to improve discipline and the rational control of feelings;
6. provide inmates with the skills they need to function within their environment and prepare for their transition to society; and
7. provide the materials and direction for implementation of learned skills.

I. Definition
    A. Secular definition
        1. Feelings of extreme displeasure, hostility, or indignation
        2. Rage or wrath toward someone or something
        3. Indignation in response to a person or situation
    B. Scriptural definition
        1. Unregenerate life of the flesh (Gal 5:19–20)
        2. Possibly sin (Mt 5:21–22)
II. Natural emotion
    A. Universal and life-long
        1. A "working through" process
        2. Does not immediately dissipate
        3. Has negative and positive aspects
    B. Positive aspects
        1. Relating to injustice and unrighteousness (Ex 2:11–12; 32:19–29)
            a) Only valid reason
            b) Self-examination and caution necessary
            c) Least common cause for anger
                (1)   False perceptions and beliefs
        2. Catalyst for reflection and positive change
        3. Tool for creativity
    C. Negative factors
        1. When anger controls (Gn 4:3–8)
            a) Develops without reflection (2 Sm 12:1–6)
            b) No "working through" process
        2. Internalized
            a) Repression
            b) Suppression
        3. Long-lasting
        4. Inappropriate ventilation
        5. Projection
        6. Displacement
        7. Disproportionate to the offense or situation (Est 3:1–6)
        8. Developing for the wrong reasons
    D. Degrees of anger
        1. Mild annoyance
        2. Violent rage
        3. Long-lasting
        4. Conscious or unconscious

III. Destructive anger
  A. Characteristics
    1. Pride (2 Kgs 5:9–14)
      a) Many causes and extensions
      b) Reap what we sow
    2. False sense of power
      a) Distortion and false security
      b) Positive power in Holy Spirit
    3. Elements of sin
      a) Jealousy (Gn 37:3–4; Prv 6:34)
      b) Unforgiveness
      c) Prejudice
      d) Bitterness and selfish ambition (Jas 3:14)
      e) Hatred (Prv 10:12; 1 Jn 3:15)
      f) Vengeance (Mt 5:38–44)
      g) Evil talk (Jas 3:8)
    4. Addictive and uncontrollable (Prv 17:14)
      a) Becomes normal reaction
      b) Resists control
      c) Lasting effects (Eccl 7:9)
      d) Influences others (Prv 22:24–25)
  B. Instruments
    1. Vengeance (Jgs 15:1–8; 16:28–30; 2 Chr 16:7–10)
    2. Aggression
      a) Verbal (1 Sm 20:30)
      b) Physical (Jgs 14:19)
    3. Withdrawal or avoidance (1 Kgs 21:1–4)
    4. Negative attitudes (Gn 27:41)
    5. Ridicule and judgment (Neh 4:1)
    6. Refusal to cooperate (2 Chr 26:16–21)
    7. Negative behavior to embarrass or injure (2 Sm 10:1–5)
    8. Gossip and slander
    9. Deliberate failures
    10. Wishing others to fail
IV. Biblical examples
  A. Hebrew Scriptures
    1. Cain's anger (Gn 4:3–7)
    2. Pharaoh toward Moses (Ex 10:11–28)
    3. Moses toward Israel (Ex 32:19; Nm 20:10)
    4. Jonah regarding Nineveh (Jon 4)

B. Christian Scriptures
   1. Herod when deceived (Mt 2:16)
   2. Disciples against James and John (Mt 20:20–28)
   3. Christ against self-righteousness (Mk 3:1–5)
   4. Herodias toward John the Baptist (Mk 6:14–19)
   5. Jesus toward his disciples (Mk 10:13–15)
   6. Christ in the temple (Mk 11:15–17)
C. Examination of biblical examples
   1. Setting
   2. Circumstances
   3. People involved
   4. Response
   5. Justification
   6. Provide positive responses
V. Christian Scripture exhortations
   A. To the Corinthians (2 Cor 12:20)
   B. Paul's pleas (Col 3:8; 1 Tm 2:8)
   C. No place in leadership (Ti 1:7)
   D. Against bitterness and revenge (Rom 12:19; Heb 12:15)
   E. No judging (Mt 7:1–5; Rom 14:4)
   F. Against every form of malice (Eph 4:31)
VI. Responses to anger (1 Kgs 21:1–13) (all elements included)
   A. Negative behavior
      1. Attitudes, communications
      2. Avoidance
      3. Slander, gossip (Prv 10:18)
      4. Criminal acts (Prv 29:22)
   B. Internalized
      1. Repression
         a) Unconscious denial
         b) Produces inner conflict
            (1) Psychological and emotional
            (2) Physical
            (3) Spiritual
            (4) Relational and other extensions
      2. Suppression
         a) Conscious exclusion
         b) Deliberate falsehood (Prv 10:18)
         c) Same effects as repression
         Note: Internalized anger will ultimately surface in one or more forms.

    C. Escapism
        1. Work or pleasures
        2. Withdrawal and exclusions
        3. Illegal activity
        4. Energy directed and concentrated elsewhere
    D. Projection and displacement
        1. Inappropriate shifts and emphasis
            a) Toward family and significant others
            b) Other substitutes
            c) Prevents self-examination
    E. Expression
        1. Sharing with family or friends
        2. Professional counsel
        3. Caution to be observed
    F. Repentance and confession
        1. To God and others (Jas 5:16; 1 Jn 1:9)
        2. Brings healing and peace
        3. Continued victory (1 Cor 10:13)
        Note: There is crossover between these responses.
VII. Reasons for not confronting anger
    A. Pride and other areas of sin (Prv 21:24; 1 Jn 2:16)
    B. Admitting to weakness or failures
    C. Self-righteousness
    D. Pleasure in nursing anger
    E. Vehicle for attention
    F. Eliminates self-examination
    G. Tool for revenge and punishment of others
VIII. Results of unrighteous anger
    A. Prevents righteousness
        1. Thoughts, attitudes, words
        2. Desires and actions
        3. Produces strife (Prv 30:33)
        4. Leads to evil (Ps 37:8)
        5. Dissension and sin (Prv 29:22)
        6. Leads others to sin (Prv 16:29)
        7. Foothold for Satan (Eph 4:26–27)
        8. Can affect salvation (Gal 5:19–21)
    B. Personal effects
        1. Psychological and emotional
        2. Physical

3. Spiritual
4. Inefficiency
5. Develops enemies
6. Affects strength and fortitude (Prv 25:28)
7. Produces foolishness (Prv 14:17, 29)
8. Addresses hope (Prv 29:20)
9. Brings judgment (Gn 49:7; Jb 19:29; Mt 5:22; Jas 5:9)
10. Kills (Jb 5:2)
    a) Spiritual
    b) Relational
    c) Emotional
    d) Opportunities
    e) Overall growth
IX. God's anger
   A. Arises from his essence
      1. Vengeance belongs to God (Rom 12:19)
        a) Never misinterprets
        b) Perfect timing
        c) Proper focus and degree (Ps 103:8–9)
        d) In love and always justified (Ps 9:8; Is 12:1)
        e) For a higher purpose (Is 55:8–9)
        f) Consistent and controlled (Am 1, 2)
        g) Against unrighteousness and injustice (Ps 2:5–9; 95:10–11; Am 5:18–20; Nah 1:2, 3, 6–8)
   B. Wrath against Christ
      1. Judicial
      2. Sacrificial love (Jn 15:12–14; Rom 5:8)
      3. Removes wrath from sinner (Rom 5:8–9)
   C. Present wrath toward unrepentance
      1. Not full expression
      2. Complete justice temporarily withheld (Ps 10; 73; 130:3–4; Is 48:9; Dn 9:9; 2 Pt 3:9)
   D. Future wrath
      1. Storing up wrath for judgment (Rom 2:5)
      2. Coming wrath of Christ (1 Thes 1:10)
      3. Final judgment (Rv 6)
X. Human anger
   A. Natural emotion
      1. God-given
      2. Not sinful in itself

    3. Reaction to unrighteousness and injustice

    4. Necessary for positive change

    5. Can be sinful and destructive

  B. Biblical warnings

    1. Acts of sinful nature (Gal 5:19–21)

    2. Easily provoked (Eccl 7:9)

    3. Work through immediately (Eph 4:26, 31)

    4. Rid self of anger (Col 3:8)

    5. Affects righteousness (Jas 1:19–20)

    6. Influences others (Prv 22:24–25)

    7. Brings judgment (Mt 5:22)

      Note: There is power in control (Prv 16:32).

  C. Difficulties of human anger

    1. Destructive if not biblical

    2. Justified through rationalization

    3. Imperfect vision

    4. Self-interest

    5. Pride, jealousy, and resentment

    6. Problem separating incident from person

XI. Reasons for anger

  A. Actions of others

    1. Real or perceived

    2. Latent or overt

    3. Criticism, judgment

    4. Personal exposure

    5. Unrealistic or unfair expectations

    6. Thwarted self-expression

    7. One or more obstacles

    8. Influences (Eph 6:4)

    9. Relational difficulties

    10. Authority issues

    11. Family of origin problems

  B. Personal causes

    1. Distorted or false perceptions

      a) Concerning situations or people

      b) Institutional, social, political

        Note: Interpretations affect emotions.

    2. Feeling vulnerable or threatened

    3. Loss of control or free will

      a) Especially for controlling personalities

4. Insecurity and self-esteem struggles
5. Real or perceived mistakes or failures
6. False understanding of failure
7. Self-fulfilling prophecies
    a) By self or others
8. Results of personal sin (Prv 6:32–34)
9. Immaturity
    a) Few coping mechanisms
    b) Lack of discipline and control (Prv 12:16)
    c) Problem with patience
    d) Low self-esteem
    e) Lack of objectivity
    f) Inability to analyze and assess
10. Personality
    a) Sensitive to frustration and injustice
    b) Familial, social, and cultural factors
    c) Expressive of emotions
11. Guilt
    a) Not expressed and worked through
12. Blocked self-will (2 Chr 25:5–10)
13. Life situation, predestination (Jb 3)
14. Lost opportunities
15. Health problems
16. Limitations
    a) Educational
    b) Social
    c) Economic
    d) Employment
17. Unmet expectations
    a) God and church
    b) Family and friends
    c) Institutional, professional
    d) Educational, social, economic, political, or
    professional
    Note: The higher the expectation, the more
    intense the anger. Perfectionism is also a con-
    sideration.
18. Obstacles or blocked goals
    a) Event, person, physical barriers

goal, the size of the obstacle, and the duration of
the frustration.

Note: Unresolved inner conflict often results in
projection, transference, or displacement.

XII. Spiritual results
   A. Grieves the Holy Spirit (Eph 4:30–31)
   B. Affects spiritual growth
      1. Repentance and confession
      2. Relationships
      3. Forgiveness (Mt 6:14–15; 18:21–22)
         a) Vertical
         b) Horizontal
      4. Hinders worship (Mt 5:23–24)
      5. Can affect salvation (Gal 5:19–21)
XIII. Prevention and control of anger
   A. Necessary measures
      1. Desire for change (Eph 4:26–32)
      2. Elimination of hostility (Prv 15:1, 18)
      3. Seek specific causes
      4. Immediate response necessary
      5. Continued self-examination
      6. Discipline required (Jas 1:19)
      7. Recognition of spiritual warfare (Eph 6:10–12)
      8. Need for divine intervention
      9. Goal is control (Prv 16:32; 25:28)
   B. Cognitive
      1. Honest self-examination
      2. Identify feelings
      3. Source or causes
      4. Justification
      5. Denial and excuses
      6. Involvement and effect on others
      7. Necessary changes
      8. Eliminate negative reflection (Prv 17:9; Eph 4:26)
      9. Focus on positives (Phil 4:4–11)
   C. Restraint (Prv 29:11)
      1. God's command (Lv 20:7, 26)
      2. Fruit of the Spirit (Gal 5:18–25)
         a) Prayer necessary

      3. Think before acting (Jas 1:19)

      4. Slow to speak and act (Jas 1:19)

      5. Relax and pause

      6. Gentle answers (Prv 15:1)

      7. Put off old habits

D. Consider results

      1. Individual, relational, and collective (Prv 29:8–9)

      2. Present, ongoing, and future

      3. Emotional and spiritual (Am 1:11–12)

E. Acceptance

      1. Unchangeable situations and circumstances

      2. One's life situation (Mt 6:34)

         a) Contentment needed (Phil 4:11–13)

      3. Imperfections in others (Mt 7:1–5)

      4. Diversity and differences (1 Cor 12:12–14)

      5. Imperfections in self (Rom 3:10; 3:23; 1 Jn 1:8)

F. Avoidance

      1. Angry people and situations (Prv 22:24–25)

         a) Seek positive models

      2. Practice emotional distancing

      3. Drugs and alcohol

G. Expectations

      1. Be realistic

         a) Regarding self and others

         b) Church and institutions

         c) Society

         d) Professions

         e) Goals and objectives

      2. Eliminate unrealistic expectations

      3. Clear perspectives and priorities

         Note: Contentment comes from within.

H. Elimination of guilt

      1. Real guilt through repentance and faith (2 Cor 7:10)

      2. Placed by others

         a) False or unrealistic

      3. Self-guilt (Rom 8:1)

         Note: Guilt causes inner conflict and anger.

 I. Flexibility

      1. Restructure when and where necessary

         a) Barriers and roles

   b) Work and goals

   c) Environment, situation, and friends

  2. Inviting change when needed

  3. Understanding necessity and positive aspects of change

  4. Recognizing that change is inevitable

J. Financial

  1. Maintain perspective

  2. Live within means

  3. Biblical understanding of stewardship

K. Ministry to self

  1. Quality time

   a) Rest and pleasure

  2. Diet and exercise

  3. Fellowship (Heb 10:25)

  4. Learn to laugh at self

  5. Less serious

  6. Develop spiritual life

L. Responsibility and accountability

  1. Acknowledgment and acceptance

  2. Eliminate projection

  3. Move toward solutions

   Note: Responsibility removes inner and relational conflict.

M. Sensitivity toward others

  1. Assume the other's place

  2. Reflection concerning reasons for attitudes and behavior of others

   a) Trials and circumstances

   b) Limitations

   c) Overall stress

  3. Understanding and compassion

   a) Eliminates anger

N. Serving others

  1. Removes attention from self

  2. Become insightful and more objective

  3. Improved understanding of life and relationships

O. Counsel

  1. With family, friends, and professionals

  2. Ventilation releases stress

  3. Enables dissipation

      4. Input and other viewpoints

      5. Brings objectivity

  P. Redirect energy

      1. Work or school

      2. Activities and hobbies

      3. Friendships

      4. Travel

  Q. Relational

      1. Truth spoken in love (Eph 4:15; 1 Pt 4:11)

      2. Share at feeling level (Mt 18:15)

      3. Communicate the issue, not the anger (Eph 4:25–26)

      4. Forgiveness necessary

      5. Maintain sensitivity and objectivity

      6. Gentle responses (Prv 12:18; 15:1)

      7. Peacemaker (Prv 15:18; Mt 5:9)

      8. Overlook insults and offenses (Prv 12:16; 19:11)

      9. Maintain perspective

      10. Acceptance of others and situations

  R. Inferiority

      1. Problems of insecurity

         a) Self-esteem and confidence

      2. Positive self-concept needed

      3. God's love emphasized

         a) Purpose of incarnation

         b) Atoning work of Christ

         c) Adoption benefits

         d) God's personal plan

         e) Covenant promises

         f) Future hope

  S. Spiritual life

      1. Acknowledgment of anger

         a) Honest self-examination

         b) Estrangement produces obligations

      2. Repentance and confession (1 Jn 1:9)

         a) To God (Mt 6:12)

         b) Others concerned (Jas 5:16)

      3. Forgiveness

         a) From God

         b) By others

       c) Toward others (Prv 17:9; Mt 5:23–24;
          Rom 12:18; Heb 12:14)
       d) Willingness to receive forgiveness
    4. Elements of forgiveness
       a) Prayerful process
       b) Necessary for reconciliation
       c) No assumptions concerning forgiveness
       d) Restitution when possible
       e) Salvation issue
    5. Scripture
       a) Provides answers
       b) Perspectives and insights
       c) Understanding and compassion develops
       d) Revelation of God's will and mission
       e) Personal transformation and power
       f) Inner peace
    6. Prayer
       a) Regarding the situation
       b) For the person
       c) For a forgiving heart (Lk 17:3–4)
       d) Continued discernment
    7. Develop nature of Christ (Phil 2:3–7)
       a) Love enemies (Lv 19:17–18; 1 Pt 4:8)
       b) Spirit controlled
       c) Predictable spiritual growth
       d) Elimination of hostility
    8. Spiritual influences
       a) Positive and negative results
          (1) Training and control
       b) Self-control a fruit of the Spirit
       c) Issues of guilt and denial
       d) Taught to repress anger
       e) Adaptation to religious groups
XIV. Modeling
  A. Christian example and growth
    1. Repentance and faith
    2. New life in Christ
    3. Love and attitudes
    4. Deeds and behavior
    5. Revelation of potential and hope

    B. Biblical exhortations
       1. Paul to Timothy—example to believers (1 Tm 4:12)
       2. Paul to Titus—example of good deeds, pure doctrine (Ti 2:7–8)
       3. Imitate conduct and faith of leaders (Heb 13:7)
       4. Universal epistle—example of prophets (Jas 5:10)
       5. To scattered Christians and elders—example to the flock (1 Pt 5:2–3)
    C. God's call
       1. To holy living (Lv 11:44–45; 19:2)
       2. Be perfect in love (Mt 5:43–48; Jn 13:34–35)
       3. Be merciful (Lk 6:36)
       4. No partiality (Eph 6:9; Acts 10:34)
    D. Example of Christ
       1. Walking in his example (1 Jn 2:6)
       2. Servanthood (Mk 10:43–45; Lk 22:27; Jn 13:13–15; 2 Cor 8:9)
       3. Acceptance of others, mind of Christ (Rom 15:2–7)
       4. Gentleness (2 Cor 10:1)
       5. Humility, attitude, and servanthood (Phil 2:5–8)
       6. Forgiveness and tolerance (Col 3:13)
       7. Love and sacrifice (Jn 15:13; Eph 5:1–2; 1 Jn 3:16)
       8. Patience (1 Tm 1:16)
       9. Faith, sacrifice, and strength (Heb 12:2–3)
      10. Called to suffering (1 Pt 2:21; 4:1)
      11. Endurance and victory (Rv 3:21)
    E. Paul's example
       1. Attitude and lifestyle (Phil 3:17; 4:9)
       2. Not exceeding what is written (1 Cor 4:6)
       3. Imitators and example to believers (1 Thes 1:6–7)
       4. Blameless behavior (1 Thes 2:10–12)
       5. Imitators of Paul's examples (1 Cor 11:1; 2 Tm 3:10)
       6. Sound words and faith in love
       7. Serving others (Acts 20:35)
XV. Dynamics of the incarcerated
    A. Themes
       1. Developmental nature
       2. Family of origin roots and influences
       3. Inadequate support systems
       4. Relational difficulties

     5. Authority issues

     6. Perceived failures and mistakes

     7. Environmental factors

     8. Educational struggles

     9. Anger and depression

    10. Inner conflict and stress

    11. Poor self-image

    12. Anxiety and uncertainty concerning the future

B. Multiple and complex

     1. Many elements and extensions

     2. Enmeshment with other factors

     3. Difficult to understand

     4. Lack of substantial resources

C. Intense

     1. Accumulative

     2. Unresolved issues

     3. Expression sought

     4. Stress of incarceration

D. Projection and displacement

     1. Family and friends

     2. Society

     3. System

     4. Institutional

E. Self-directed anger

     1. Wrong decisions and failure

     2. Strained family and other relationships

     3. Loss of opportunities

     4. Addictions

     5. Struggles with pride and forgiveness

F. Institutional

     1. Stress factors

     2. Dehumanizing experience

     3. Lack of incentives

     4. Attitudes of the administration

     5. Categorization

     6. Attitudes of peers

     7. Lack of honest relationships

     8. Few opportunities and rehabilitative tools

G. Family
   1. Lack of understanding and forgiveness
   2. Suspicion and mistrust
   3. Insufficient support
H. Survival responses
   1. Attitude development and philosophy
   2. Defense and coping mechanisms—power
   3. Role play
   4. Resources

C

Christian Unity

This outline is designed to provide a biblical understanding of diversity in the context of God's unifying love, with an emphasis on the ministry and teachings of Jesus Christ. It should

1. provide liberation from the ignorance that produces prejudice and division;
2. facilitate an understanding of the divine purpose for unity;
3. improve fellowship within the body of Christ by encouraging a community spirit that fosters mutual support, healing, and service;
4. examine unity in terms of the eschatological future; and
5. develop an ecumenical witness.

I. Definition
   A. Oneness of sentiment, affections, and purpose (Rom 12:15–16)
   B. Unanimity of belief, specifically in Christ (1 Cor 1:10)
   C. Unity of faith, being one in Christ (2 Cor 13:11; Eph 4:1–6, 11–13)
   D. Hebrew Scripture acknowledgment (Ps 133; Is 52:7–8)
II. Biblical attributes
   A. Sharing, mutual edification, equal concern, and intercession (Rom 12:15–16; 14:19; 1 Cor 12:25; Gal 6:2; Phil 2:1–2; Jas 5:16)
   B. One in spirit and purpose, like-minded, having the same love (Rom 15:5–6; 1 Cor 10:17; 12:13; Phil 2:2)
   C. Attitude of Christ—servanthood (Eph 4:15–16; 5:21–25; Phil 2:3–8; 1 Pt 2:15–18)
   D. Harmony, one in heart, mind, and thought—no conceit (Acts 4:32; Rom 12:16; 1 Cor 1:10)
   E. Living in peace (Rom 12:18; 2 Cor 13:11–12; Eph 4:1–3; 1 Tm 2:1–2)
III. Characteristics of unconditional love
   A. Humble, patient, bearing with one another in love (Eph 4:1–3; 5:2; Col 2:2; 1 Thes 3:12)
   B. Encouragement, help, patience, kindness (even to enemies), and service (1 Thes 5:11–15; Heb 3:12–13; 10:24–25)
   C. Harmony, sympathy, humility, compassion, and love as brothers (1 Pt 3:8)
   D. Hospitality (1 Pt 4:8–10)
   E. Paul's summary (1 Cor 13)
IV. Witness through unity (Jn 13:35; 15:27; Acts 22:15)
   A. Proof of God's power and love (Eph 2:19–22)
   B. Revelation and confirmation of the gospel (1 Jn 3:14; 4:11–13; Acts 2:1–4)
   C. Draws people to Christ (Jn 13:34–35; 15:19)
   D. Undivided strength against evil
   E. Strong force for mission (Jn 17:20–23)
V. Essence of unity
   A. Spiritual entity dependent upon God
   B. Spirit of unity (Ps 133:1; Eph 4:1–3)
      1. One heart and voice for God's glorification (Acts 4:32; Rom 15:5–6)

      2. Agreement, united in mind and thought (1 Cor 1:10; Phil 1:27)

      3. Living in peace with one mind (2 Cor 13:11; 1 Thes 5:12–13; 1 Pt 3:8)

  C. Not unanimity in perception

      1. Exists in diversity (1 Cor 12:12–13)

      2. Different parts—all vital (1 Cor 12:14–26)

         a) Even the smallest parts—those considered to be insignificant

      3. Benefits in diversity (1 Cor 12:4–11; 27–31)

  D. Institutional characteristics

      1. Gifts bring ministry—mutual support, encouragement, bonding, and healing (Eph 4:11–16)

      2. Fellowship unites (Heb 10:24–25)

      3. Stability and identity (1 Pt 4:10–11)

      4. Unity through images and symbols (1 Cor 10:16–17)

      5. Oneness through creeds and confessions (Acts 4:23–31; 1 Cor 15:1–6)

      6. Unification in doctrine and polity

  E. Sacraments

      1. United profession and proclamation (Jn 13:8–9; 1 Cor 10:1–2)

      2. Vertical and horizontal unity

      3. Eschatological significance (Rv 19:7–10)

VI. Hebrew Scripture basis

  A. Unity in the triune God (Dt 6:4)

      1. The will of the Trinity (Gn 1:26)

      2. Seen in God's essence, creating acts, fellowship, love, and purpose

  B. Created order

      1. Reveals unity and interdependence

  C. Human life

      1. God's image (Gn 1:27)

      2. Fellowship with humanity (Gn 2:18–25)

      3. Promises and covenants (Gn 9:16; 12:2–3; Dt 30:1–10; 2 Chr 7:14)

      4. Continued presence and calling

         a) Forgiveness and providence (Jgs 3:8–11)

         b) Overall ministry

      5. Pre-incarnate Christ (Gn 12:7; 17:1–2; 18:1, 22; 26:2; Jos 5:13–15)

VII. Unity through proclamation

   A. Experienced in the calling

      1. One message (Mt 28:19–20; Lk 24:47; Jn 10:14–16; Acts 1:8; Rom 1:16–17)

      2. Called to one repentance (Ez 33:11; Mt 23:37; Mk 1:14–15; 2 Pt 3:9)

      3. Universal atonement (Is 53; Jn 3:16)

      4. One flock and kingdom (Ps 100; Jn 10:1–16)

      5. One Resurrection hope (Jn 11:25–26; 2 Cor 5:6–10; Phil 1:21–24; Heb 9:27–28)

   B. Message of reconciliation (Is 52:7; 61:1–3; Lk 4:18–19)

      1. Universal peace (Na 1:15; Mt 5:9; Rom 14:19; 2 Cor 13:11)

      2. Good news to the poor (Is 61:1; Lk 4:18)

         a) Includes poor in spirit (Mt 5:3)

      3. Freedom from sin (Jn 8:34)

         a) Freedom from alienation

         b) Freedom for a new life (Jn 8:31, 32, 36; 2 Cor 5:17)

         c) Liberated to love (Mt 5:43–48; Mk 12:28–31; Lk 6:27–36; Jn 13:34–35)

   C. Universal proclamation

      1. Kingdom touches everyone (Mk 1:14–15)

      2. Response required (Mk 1:15)

   D. Institutional church

      1. Liberation (Jn 8:31–32)

         a) Makes proclamation possible

         b) Establishes and reinforces truth (Mt 18:15–20; Acts 15:1–35)

      2. All communications significant

         a) A witness (1 Cor 3:5–10; 10:32–33)

         b) Positive witness unites (Jn 13:1–17; Gal 1:6–14; 2 Thes 3:7–8; 1 Tm 4:12; 1 Pt 2:20–25)

VIII. Unity through reconciliation (2 Cor 5:14–21)

   A. Christ's love compels (verse 14)

   B. Universal atonement—all died (verse 14)

   C. Live for God and others (verse 15)

   D. Understand others from God's view (verse 16)

E. New creation in Christ (verse 17)

F. Reconciled through Christ (verse 18)

G. Ministry of reconciliation (verses 18, 19)

H. Ambassadors of Christ (verse 20)

IX. Unifying work of the Holy Spirit

    A. Unites creation with Father and Son

    B. One creation from diversity (1 Cor 10:17; 12:4–31)

    C. Unites all things in him (Eph 4:4, 11–13)

    D. Calls everyone to Christ (Heb 3:7–8)

        1. Conviction (Jn 16:7–11; Acts 2:36–39)

        2. Repentance (Acts 3:17–19; 11:15–18)

        3. Regeneration (Ez 36:24–27; 37:1–14; Jn 3:5–6; 1 Cor 6:19; 2 Cor 5:17; Ti 3:5)

        4. Indwelling (Acts 10:44–45; 1 Cor 3:16; 6:19; Eph 2:22; 2 Tm 1:14; 1 Jn 2:27)

        5. Baptism of Holy Spirit (Mt 3:11; Acts 1:4–8; Rom 6:1–10; 1 Cor 12:13; Gal 3:26–28; Col 2:9–12)

            a) Pentecost (Acts 2:1–13, 41)

                (1) Different tongues for one message (Acts 2:4–11)

                (2) Drawn into common life, spirit, and ministry (Acts 2:42–47)

        6. Reconciliation (Rom 5:7–11; Eph 2:13–18)

            a) One forgiveness and acceptance (2 Cor 5:14–21)

            b) One adoption with its benefits (Jn 1:12; Rom 8:1, 14–17; Gal 3:28–29; 4:4–7)

            c) One family (Mt 12:50; Jn 10:16; Heb 2:11)

X. Unity through Christ

    A. Incarnation (Mt 1:18–25)

        1. God uniting with humanity (Is 7:14; Ez 36:26–27; Lk 1:31–33; 1 Tm 3:16; 1 Jn 4:2)

    B. Ministry of Christ

        1. Teachings and example (Mt 4:23–25; Col 3:1 6–17)

        2. United in Christ's death (Jn 10:11; Rom 5:6–8)

        3. Resurrection hope (Acts 26:22–23; 1 Pt 1:3–5)

        4. High priest for all (Heb 2:17–18; 4:14–16)

    C. Second Advent

        1. Perfection of oneness

        2. Gathering of the elect (Mt 13:24–30; 24:29–31; 2 Thes 2:1–3; Heb 9:27–28)

3. One Resurrection (Rom 8:11; 1 Cor 15:20–22)
4. Eternal union with Christ and elect (Is 9:6–7;
   Lk 1:30–33; Jn 11:25–26; 14:2–3; Rom 6:8)

XI. Components of unity
  A. Examination of Ephesians 4:4–6
    1. One body and Spirit (verse 4; Rom 12:5; 1 Cor 12:27)
    2. Called to one hope (verse 4; Rom 15:4)
    3. One Lord, one faith, one baptism (verse 5; 1 Tm 2:5)
    4. One God and Father of all, who is over all and
       through all and in all (verse 6; 1 Cor 12:4–6;
       15:24–28)

XII. Unity through truth in Christ
  A. Testimony of Holy Spirit and disciples (Jn 14:16–17;
     15:26; 16:13)
  B. Truth is unifying (Jn 1:12; 17:15–22; 18:37)
  C. Unity through freedom (Lk 4:18–19; Jn 8:32, 36;
     2 Cor 3:17; Gal 5:1)
    1. Free to forgive and love (Jn 13:34–35; 15:12–13)
    2. Free from the sins that divide (Rom 6; 8:1–2)
    3. Not free to destroy freedom (Gal 5:13–15)

XIII. Universal atonement
  A. Equal and universal forgiveness (Ps 103:10–12; Is 1:18;
     55:6–7; 1 Tm 2:5–6; 1 Jn 2:1–2)
    1. None are worthless (Rom 3:21–30; 5:6–10)
    2. God's desire that none be lost (2 Pt 3:9)
      a) Example: Parable of the Lost Sheep (Mt 18:10–14)
  B. All reconciled (2 Cor 5:17–19)
  C. United in Resurrection hope (1 Cor 15:20–23)

XIV. Unity with Christ establishes unity with others
  A. Fruit minimizes differences (Jn 15:4–9, 16–17;
     Gal 5:22–26; Eph 5:8–9)
  B. Gifts deepen unity (Rom 12:4–10; 1 Cor 12:4–10;
     Eph 4:11–13; 1 Pt 4:10)
  C. Service unifies (1 Cor 9:18–23)
  D. Unity through maturity (Eph 4:11–16)
    1. Growth eliminates divisions (1 Cor 1:14–17)
    2. Creates objectivity and understanding
    3. Barriers break down (Acts 10:28; 1 Cor 1:27–30)
    4. Diversity becomes growth

XV. Community life
  A. Brings people together in unity (Acts 1:12–14; 2:1, 42–47;
     Rom 1:7; 1 Cor 1:2)
     1. Jesus' prayer for oneness (Jn 17:20–23)
     2. Paul's prayer for unity (Rom 15:5–12)
     3. Christian Scripture fellowship (Acts 2:42–47; 4:32;
        11:27–30)
     4. Fellowship important (Heb 10:24–25)
     5. One family (Mt 12:50; Jn 10:16; Heb 2:11)
     6. Sense of identity (Jn 17:20–21; Acts 2:42;
        1 Cor 10:16–17; 12:12–13)
  B. Undivided entity of the new creation (Rom 15:5–7;
     2 Cor 5:17–18; Phil 2:1–2)
     1. Support system through trials (Acts 12:1–17; Jas 1:27)
     2. A giving community (1 Cor 16:1–3; 2 Cor 8:7–14, 24)
     3. Meeting needs (Acts 4:32–35; 20:35; Rom 15:1–2;
        Eph 4:28; 1 Thes 5:11, 14, 15)
     4. Carry each other's burdens (2 Cor 9:1–15; Gal 6:2)
     5. Live in harmony, identify with feelings, no partiality,
        love enemies (Rom 12:14–17)
     6. Special love relationship (Gal 6:10)
     7. Oneness in diversity (Rom 12:3–10; 1 Cor 1:10;
        12:4–13; Eph 4:3–6)
     8. Like-minded, same love, one in spirit and purpose,
        humility, consider others better, look to interests of
        others, same attitude as Christ, servanthood, sacrifice
        (Phil 2:1–8)
     9. Sympathy, love as brothers, compassion, love of
        enemies (1 Pt 3:8–9)
     10. Love, hospitality, gifts for service, Godly
        communications (1 Pt 4:8–11)
     11. Christ is all and in all (1 Cor 12:6; Col 3:11)
     12. No lordship or slavery (Mt 20:25–28; 1 Pt 5:1–3)
     13. All equal in Christ (Rom 10:12–13; Gal 3:26–29)
  C. Precedes birth and extends beyond death
     1. Rooted in Christ's apostles (1 Cor 3:10–11;
        Eph 2:19–22)
     2. Christ greater than differences (Acts 2:44;
        Eph 2:11–22)
     3. No limits or bounds

      4. Communion of people in Christ (Mt 18:20)

      5. Includes the church triumphant (1 Thes 4:13–18)

      6. Eschatological implications (1 Cor 6:2–3; Rv 5:8–10)

   D. Biblical images of affirmation

      1. Chosen people, royal priesthood, holy nation, people belonging to God, spiritual house (1 Pt 2:5–10; Rv 20:6)

      2. Bride of Christ (Rv 19:7; 21:9)

      3. Body of Christ (1 Cor 12:27; Eph 1:22–23; Col 1:12–18, 24)

      4. One flock (Jn 10:16; Acts 20:28)

      5. New creation (2 Cor 5:17; Eph 2:11–22; Col 3:10–11)

      6. Temple (1 Cor 3:16–17)

      7. Holy City, New Jerusalem (Heb 13:10–14; Rv 21:2; 22:19)

   E. Earthly form of Christ's ministry

      1. Through the Word (Jn 5:24)

      2. Sanctified life

         a) Alternative to the world (Rom 12:1–2; Jas 4:4; 1 Jn 2:15–17)

         b) Attraction through love (1 Cor 13; 1 Jn 4:7–20)

      3. Utilization of gifts (Rom 12:3–8; 1 Pt 4:10–11)

         a) To build up the body (Eph 4:11–16)

         b) For common good (1 Cor 12:7–11)

      4. Priestly intercession

         a) Through prayer (Eph 3:14–21; 6:18; Col 1:9; 2 Thes 1:11–12; Jas 5:13–15)

         b) Renovate fallen world (Mt 5:13–16; 2 Cor 5:11–21)

         c) Healing community (2 Cor 1:3–6)

      5. Individual and collective strength (Eph 4:14–16; 6:10)

         a) Deepens faith and worship

         b) Quickens sense of mission

XVI. Equality brings unity

   A. Community of equals (Prv 22:2; Mt 23:8; Rom 10:12; 1 Cor 12:13; Gal 3:28–29)

      1. In faith and pardon (Acts 11:18; Rom 3:23–24; Gal 3:22–29)

      2. Rights and dignity (Rom 2:11; Eph 6:9)

      3. Equal in fellowship (1 Cor 12:13; Phil 1:3–6; 1 Jn 1:7)

B. No distinctions
  1. Human identity without barriers (1 Cor 7:17–24; Eph 2:14–22)
  2. Spirit of acceptance (Rom 15:7; Gal 2:9)
  3. No depreciation of others (Mk 9:38–40)
  4. Acceptance of others in their "otherness" (Mt 15:21–28; Jn 4:6–9; Acts 10:28; 11:1–18)
  5. Faith in God's forgiveness of oneself
    a) Justification of self before others
    b) Eliminates ego identification before others
XVII. Serving brings unity
  A. Removes attention from self (Mt 16:24–25)
    1. Enables seeing others (1 Cor 10:33; Phil 2:3–5)
    2. Develops understanding and compassion (Mt 15:32–38)
  B. God's will (Rom 12:20; 15:1–3; Gal 5:13–14)
  C. Example: servanthood of Christ (Lk 22:27; Jn 13:4–5; Phil 2:1–8)
  D. Greatest is servant of all (Mt 20:25–27; 23:11; Lk 22:25–27)
    1. Involvement with humanity
    2. Humility and sacrifice
  E. Extent of servanthood (Mt 5:40–42; 10:7–8, 41–42; 25:31–46; Jn 12:23–26)
XVIII. Mutual dependency brings unity
  A. One humanity reflecting the same needs
  B. Vine and branches (Jn 15:1–6)
    1. Different branches—size and foliage (1 Cor 12:4–6; Eph 4:11–13)
    2. All branches dependent upon vine (2 Cor 3:5)
    3. One vine nourishes (Jn 4:6–15; 6:47–51; 15:15)
    4. Unity through the vine (Rom 12:4–5)
    5. All branches contribute and make up the vine (Rom 12:6–8)
  C. One body with many parts (1 Cor 12:12–31)
    1. Many form one (verse 12)
    2. Baptized by one Spirit into one body (verse 13; Eph 4:4–5)

3. Needed parts arranged by God (verses 18, 19; 1 Cor 12:6; Eph 4:16)
    a) Includes the seemingly weak (verses 22, 23; 1 Cor 1:27–28)
    b) Includes those not visible (verse 23)
4. No divisions (verse 25; Acts 10:34)
5. All gifts needed (verses 27–31)

XIX. Sacrament of baptism as sign and profession
  A. By one Spirit into one body (1 Cor 12:13)
  B. All baptized into Christ (Gal 3:27–28)
    1. One in Christ and Abraham's seed (Rom 2:28–29; 4:1–16)
  C. United into Christ's death and resurrection
    1. Has ethical extensions (Rom 6:1–10)
  D. Liberated into a new humanity
    1. Free from power of sin (Rom 6:6–14)
    2. No barriers, divisions, or status (1 Cor 12:13)
    3. Free to understand God's liberation
  E. Christ's union through his baptism (Mt 3:13–17)
    1. Identification with universal proclamation
    2. Identification with sinners
  F. Commission and command through baptism (Mt 28: 19–20)

XX. Eucharist
  A. Unity in Messianic fellowship (Mk 14:22–26)
  B. Universal bond with kingdom (1 Cor 10:17)
    1. Present and future aspects
    2. Anticipation of future unity (Mt 26:26–29)
  C. Self-giving of Christ
    1. Universal atonement—died for all, including enemies (Rom 5:8–10; 1 Jn 4:9–10)
      a) Overcomes separation and enmity (Ti 3:1–6)
      b) Grace restoring humanity and relationships (Col 3:12–16)
  D. Participation in sacrifice and servanthood of Christ— our example (Phil 2:1–8)
    1. Enter the human situation
    2. Called into forgiving solidarity
  E. Unifying fellowship (Mt 5:21–24; 2 Cor 5:18)
    1. One bread and cup
    2. Mutual need and confession
    3. One faith, one hope

F. Reconciliation demanded (2 Cor 5:18)
1. Through self-examination and judgment in God's reconciling presence
2. Called to be servants of reconciliation
    a) Social, economic, political, and spiritual
XXI. Creeds reflect unity
A. Statements and confessions of faith
1. Essentials of Christianity
2. Apostolic and Catholic
B. Continuity and succession
1. Through Christ's apostles
2. Same Spirit, Word, and ministry
3. Same sacraments
XXII. Eschatological significance
A. Earthly church connected to future kingdom
1. Twofold aspect of the kingdom
2. Present unity foreshadows future
3. Relates to Parousia
    a) Gathering of those united
    b) One Bride and wedding feast
XXIII. Division through partiality
A. Favoritism is a sin (Jas 2:9)
B. Examples: family, friends, race, wealth, position, education, affiliations
C. Impartial God (Acts 10:34; Gal 3:28–29)
D. Servant to least (Mt 25:31–46)
XXIV. Paul's response to disunity (Gal 5:13–26)
A. Call to live in the Spirit (verse 16)
1. Produces fruit for unity
2. Examples of fruit: love, joy, peace, patience, kindness, gentleness, goodness, self-control, faithfulness (verses 22, 23)
XXV. Ecumenism
A. Definition
1. Seeking worldwide unity among religions through cooperation and understanding
2. Not a compromise of doctrine
B. Division fragments Christ (1 Cor 1:10–13)

C. Must recognize existing unity in Christ
  1. We in Christ and Christ in us
  2. One and equal in Christ
  3. Faith and love as unifying elements
D. Biblical images
  1. Universal language and oneness emphasized
  2. Examples: one body, bride, flock, temple, people of God, priesthood
  3. Jesus, Lord of all
  4. One proclamation, witness, ministry
  5. One church
    a) Room for nonessential differences
E. Requirements for ecumenism
  1. Change of heart and attitude
  2. Insight, understanding, objectivity, and faith
  3. Courage and imagination to embrace God's gifts of unity
F. Benefits
  1. Realize God's greatness
    a) Not confined to culture, geography, denominations, or circumstances
  2. Enables widest possible service
  3. Reveals unifying and transforming power
  4. Strong force against evil aggression
  5. Strength for mission
  6. Picture of God's infinite love
XXVI. Positives of diversity
  A. Experience the inclusiveness of God
    1. Enables learning and growth
      a) New associations and insights
  B. Pluralism necessitates multiple gifts
    1. Community gifts for ministry (1 Cor 12:4–12; 1 Pt 4:10–11)
    2. Enhance personal and community life
    3. Complementary
  C. Provides a healing community
    1. Mutual help, understanding, and sympathy
    2. Recycling effect of ministry
  D. Reinforce spiritual unity

XXVII. Steps toward unity
    A. Requires desire, understanding, effort, and goals
        1. Prayer (Mt 7:7–8; 21:22; Jn 15:7–8)
            a) Realization and understanding of God's will
                (Ps 40:8; 143:10; Jer 9:23–24)
            b) Spirit of oneness (Rom 12:5; Eph 4:4–6)
            c) Ability to be a witness of unity (Mt 24:14)
        2. Cultivation
            a) To practice understanding, forbearance,
                tolerance, patience, acceptance, gentleness
                (Gal 5:22–26; Eph 5:8–11)
                (1) In all environments and circumstances
                    (Eph 4:1–3)
                (2) Begins at home (Mk 7:10; Eph 5:22–33;
                    6:1–4; Col 3:18–21)
            b) Love (Jn 15:9–14)
        3. Focus on positive examples (Phil 4:8–9)
            a) Essentials (Rom 13:8)
        4. Understand greatness of God
            a) Recognize and accept providence
            b) Not to limit God's work
        5. Work toward common good (Phil 4:3)
            a) Service to others (Mk 10:42–44; Jn 13:13–17;
                Rom 16:1–2)
            b) Goals of healing and reconciliation (2 Cor 5:18)
        6. Avoid divisive attitudes (Prv 17:14; 20:3; Rom 16:17)
            a) Examples: pride, self-confidence, superiority,
                self-sufficiency, prejudice, resentment, jealousy,
                criticism, judgment, partiality (Acts 10:28)
        7. Good listener and objective thinker
XXVIII. Scripture on unity
    Ps 133
    Mt 5:9
    Jn 10:16; 17:20–23
    Acts 2:42–47; 4:32–35
    Rom 12:3–8, 15–17; 14:19; 15:5–8
    1 Cor 1:10–13; 10:16–17; 12:4–30; 2 Cor 13:11
    Gal 3:26–29; 6:2, 10
    Eph 4:1–6, 11–16
    Phil 1:27–28; 2:1–8; 3:16–17

1 Thes 5:12–15
Heb 3:12–13; 10:24–25
Jas 5:16
1 Pt 3:8; 4:8–11
1 Jn 1:3

D

Bibilical Foundations

Christian foundations are built upon strong biblical principles, such as forgiveness, adoption, grace, spiritual rest, and hope. Expounding upon these themes within their biblical context stimulates personal development. While other themes and principles are also important to spiritual formation, prison inmates find particular comfort and strength in these truths. Biblical foundations enable us to

1. understand the depth of God's forgiveness and how reconciliation is accomplished;
2. view the biblical concept of spiritual adoption, which creates a sense of being part of God's family and kingdom;
3. comprehend the fullness of grace as a divine gift that overshadows our past and present imperfections;
4. move toward a life in which spiritual rest is a reality;
5. develop an inner peace that brings stability in the midst of turmoil;
6. begin to live with the hope that is only found in Jesus Christ.

I. Forgiveness
   A. Hebrew Scriptures
      1. Sin separates (Ps 32:1–5; Is 43:24; Am 3:2; Mi 3:8)
         a) God's wrath
         b) Anxiety and fear
         c) Bondage (Hos 5:4)
         d) Out of harmony with nature and humanity
      2. Means of forgiveness
         a) Torah—Levitical system (Ex 20–23; Lv 16–27; Dt 12–26)
         b) Covenants (1 Kgs 8:30; Ps 130:3–4; Jer 31:34)
         c) Prophets (Jer 3:1; Ez 18; 37)
      3. Repentance required (Is 58:6–7; Jl 2:13)
   B. Christian Scriptures
      1. Call for repentance
         a) Baptism of repentance (Mk 1:4)
         b) Ministry of Jesus—repentance and faith (Mk 1:15)
      2. Forgiveness of others necessary (Mt 6:14; 18:23–35; Mk 11:25; Lk 11:4; 17:3)
      3. Mission of the church (2 Cor 5:18)
II. Adoption
   A. Hebrew Scriptures
      1. God's merciful election (Ex 4:22; Dt 14:2; Hos 11:1)
   B. Christian Scriptures
      1. Affected through baptism (Rom 8:15; Gal 4:6)
      2. Witness of the Holy Spirit (Rom 8:16; 1 Pt 3:21)
      3. Resources
         a) Petitions (Jn 16:23)
         b) Needs supplied (Rom.8:32; 1 Tm 6:17)
      4. Eschatological future (Rom 8:23; Rv 21:7)
         a) Heirs—receive all things (2 Cor 6:18; Gal 4:4–6; Eph 1:5)
III. Grace
   A. Hebrew Scriptures
      1. Election of Israel
         a) Exodus events
         b) Torah and covenants
         c) Remnant

B. Christian Scriptures
  1. God's gift (2 Cor 8:1; 9:14)
  2. Through Jesus Christ (Rom 3:24; 5:15; 2 Thes 1:12)
     a) Incarnation, death, and resurrection (Rom 5:9; 2 Cor 8:9; Eph 2:6)
     b) Universal atonement
        (1) Equal and universal forgiveness (Mt 20:28; 1 Tm 2:5–6; 1 Jn 2:2)
        (2) None are worthless (Rom 3:21–30; 5:6–10)
        (3) God's desire that none be lost (Mt 18:10–14; 2 Pt 3:9)
        (4) Ministry of reconciliation (2 Cor 5:18–19)
        (5) United in resurrection hope (1 Cor 15:20–21)
        (6) Salvation (Rom 3:24; 5:1; Eph 2:5)
     c) Sufficiency (2 Cor 12:9)
     d) Related to faith (Eph 2:8; Heb 4:16)
     e) Can be resisted (Gal 2:21; 5:4)
     f) Selection and gifts for service (Rom 1:5; 12:6–8; 1 Cor 15:9–10; Gal 2:9; Eph 3:7)
  3. According to Christ's apportionment (Eph 4:7)
  4. Christian Scripture theme (Mt 20:1–16; Lk 15:11–14; 18:4; Rom 6:23; 2 Cor 5:14–21)
  5. Meets human need (2 Cor 12:9)
     a) Forgiveness (Rom 3:24; 5:1–2; 6:14; Gal 2:21; 5:5–6; Eph 2:8–9)
     b) Sanctification (2 Pt 3:18)
     c) Relationships (Eph 4:29)
IV. Call to rest
  A. Hebrew Scriptures
    1. Physical rest (Ex 33:14; Dt 3:20; Jos 1:13–15)
    2. Freedom from war (Jos 23:1; 2 Sm 7:1)
    3. Sabbath rest (Ex 20:10)
    4. Political and social security (Jer 6:16)
    5. Death (Jb 3:17–19)
    Note: Canaan was an imperfect rest.
  B. Christian Scriptures
    1. Promise of Christ (Mt 11:28–29)
    2. Entering God's rest (Heb 4:11)
    3. Death as final rest (Rv 14:13)

V. Peace
  A. Hebrew Scriptures
    1. Given by God (Ps 29:11; Is 26:3)
      a) Outward tranquillity—individual and nations
        (Nm 6:26; 1 Kgs 4:24)
    2. Individual peace
      a) Health and good life (Jgs 18:6)
    3. Communal—family and nation
      a) Covenants (Lv 26:6)
      b) Prosperity and security
      c) Economic (1 Chr 4:40)
      d) Political security (2 Kgs 20:19)
      e) Military victory (Jgs 8:9)
      f) Absence of war (Jgs 21:13)
      g) Surrender (2 Sm 10:19)
      h) Treaties and agreements (Dt 2:26)
    4. Spiritual peace (Ps 119:65; Is 26:3; 52:7)
      a) Effect of righteousness (Is 32:17; 59:8)
      b) Covenants (Is 54:10; Ez 37:26)
    5. Eschatological future (Is 2:3–5; 11:6–10)
  B. Christian Scriptures
    1. God's essence (Rom 15:33)
    2. Reconciliation with God (Mt 5:9; Rom 5:1)
    3. Achieved through Christ (Lk 1:79; Jn 14:27;
       Acts 10:36; Eph 2:15)
      a) Spiritual state (Rom 8:6; 14:17; 15:13)
      b) Fruit of the Spirit (Gal 5:22)
    4. Affects relationships (Mk 9:50; Lk 2:14; 1 Thes 5:13)
      a) Christian unity (Eph 4:1–3)
      b) Peacemaker
        (1) Draw from the peace given by God
        (2) Create peace where there is hatred
        (3) Blessed by God (Mt 5:9)
VI. Hope
  A. Hebrew Scriptures
    1. Source of trust (Dt 32:4; Ps 9:10; 13:5; 18:2, 31, 46;
       62:2, 6–7; Is 26:4)
    2. Refuge and deliverance (Ps 5:11; 7:1; 14:6; 16:1; 61:3;
       73:28; 91:9; 94:22; Prv 14:26; Ez 34:27–28)
    3. Security and peace (Jb 11:18; Is 26:3)

4. Confident expectation of good (Prv 10:28)
5. Promise for the future (Ps 65:5; 71)
6. Patiently waiting for salvation (Ps 31:24; 33:18–22)

B. Christian Scriptures
  1. Pauline theology
    a) Confidence (Rom 4:18)
    b) God as source and ground of hope (Rom 15:13; Eph 4:4–6; Col 1:23)
    c) Covenant through Christ (Eph 2:2)
    d) Present reality (1 Cor 9:24–27; 1 Thes 1:3)
    e) Inheritance (Eph 1:13–18; 1 Thes 5:8)
    f) Changed through the Holy Spirit (Rom 5:5; 15:13; 1 Cor 2:9–16)
      (1) First fruit (Rom 8:23–30; Eph 1:13)
      (2) Liberty (Rom 8:21)
      (3) Image of Christ (2 Cor 3:12–18)
      (4) Share God's glory (Rom 5:2)
      (5) Righteousness (Gal 5:5)
    g) Redemption—victory over death (1 Cor 15; 1 Thes 4)
  2. Other passages
    a) Expectation of the Messiah (Lk 24:21)
    b) Mark of rebirth (1 Pt 1:3)
    c) Our resurrection (Acts 24:15; 26:6–7)
    d) Eschatological future (1 Pt 1:13, 20)

References

Aiello, John R., and Andrew Baum, eds. 1979. *Residential Crowding and Design*. New York: Plenum.

Alston, Wallace M., Jr. 1984. *Guides to the Reformed Tradition: The Church*. Atlanta: John Knox Press.

Barth, Karl. 1960a. *Doctrine of Creation, the Creature*. Vol. 3, pt. 2 of *Church Dogmatics*. Edinburgh: T. & T. Clark.

———. 1960b. *The Humanity of God*. Richmond, Va.: John Knox Press.

Birch, Bruce C., and Larry L. Rasmussen. 1989. *Bible and Ethics in the Christian Life*. Minneapolis: Augsburg Fortress.

Bonhoeffer, Dietrich. 1963. *The Cost of Discipleship*. New York: Collier Books.

Clinebell, Howard. 1984. *Basic Types of Pastoral Care and Counseling: Resources for the Ministry of Healing and Growth*. Nashville: Abingdon Press.

Collins, Gary R. 1980. *Christian Counseling*. Waco, Tex.: Word Books.

Cox, Verne C., Paul B. Paulus, Garvin McCain, and Janette K. Schkade. 1979. "Field Research on the Effects of Crowding in Prisons and Offshore Drilling Platforms." In *Residential Crowding and Design*, edited by John R. Aiello and Andrew Baum, 100–101. New York: Plenum.

Dulles, Avery. 1974. *Models of the Church*. New York: Image Books.

Ellis, Albert. 1977. *Anger: How to Live With and Without It*. Secaucus, N.J.: Citadel.

Fox, Vernon. 1956. *Violence Behind Bars*. New York: Vantage Press.

Goffman, Erving. 1967. *Interaction Ritual*. New York: Doubleday.

Hempel, Joel, and Jill Westberg. 1980. "Six Action Models of Ministry." In *Health and Healing: Ministry of the Church*, edited by Henry L. Lettermann, 117–27. Madison, Wis.: Wheat Ridge Foundation.

Hopstock, Paul J., John R. Aiello, and Andrew Baum. 1979. "Residential Crowding Research." In *Residential Crowding and Design*, edited by John R. Aiello and Andrew Baum, 9–21. New York: Plenum.

Houston, John P., Helen Bee, Elaine Hatfield, and David C. Rimm. 1979. *Invitation to Psychology*. New York: Academic Press.

Irwin, John. 1970. *The Felon*. Englewood Cliffs, N.J.: Prentice Hall.

Johnson, Susanne. 1989. *Christian Spiritual Formation in the Church and Classroom*. Nashville: Abingdon.

Kempis, Thomas à. 1966. "The Discipline of the Inner Life." In *Readings in Christian Thought*, edited by Hugh T. Kerr, 132–33. Nashville: Abingdon.

Klug, Ronald. 1982. *How to Keep a Spiritual Journal*. Nashville: Thomas Nelson.

Küng, Hans. 1976. *The Church*. Garden City, N.Y.: Image Books.

Layden, Milton. 1977. *Escaping the Hostility Trap*. Englewood Cliffs, N.J.: Prentice Hall.

Lettermann, Henry L., ed. 1980. "Task Group Reports." In *Health and Healing: Ministry of the Church*, 150–68. Madison, Wis.: Wheat Ridge Foundation.

Matza, David. 1969. *Becoming Deviant*. Englewood Cliffs, N.J.: Prentice Hall.

May, Rollo. 1972. *Power and Innocence*. New York: W. W. Norton.

McQuade, Walter, and Ann Aikman. 1974. *Stress*. New York: Bantam Books.

Miller, Roland E. 1980. "Christ the Healer." In *Health and Healing: Ministry of the Church*, edited by Henry L. Lettermann, 15–40. Madison, Wis.: Wheat Ridge Foundation.

Minirth, Frank, Don Hawkins, Paul Meir, and Richard Flournoy. 1986. *How to Beat Burnout*. Chicago: Moody Press.

Ministerial Association. 1988. General Conference of Seventh-day Adventists. *Seventh-day Adventists Believe: A Biblical Exposition of 27 Fundamental Doctrines*. Hagerstown, Md.: Ministerial Association, General Conference of Seventh-day Adventists.

Moltmann, Jurgen. 1974. *The Crucified God*. New York: Harper and Row.

―――. 1975. *The Church in the Power of the Spirit*. New York: Harper and Row.

Niebuhr, H. Richard. 1956. *The Purpose of the Church and Its Ministry*. New York: Harper and Brothers.

Ogilvie, Lloyd John. 1981. *The Beauty of Caring*. Eugene, Ore.: Harvest House.

Pattison, Stephen. 1988. *A Critique of Pastoral Care*. London: SCM Press.

Peterson, Eugene H. 1980. *Five Smooth Stones for Pastoral Work*. Atlanta: John Knox Press.

Purves, Andrew. 1989. *The Search for Compassion: Spirituality and Ministry*. Louisville, Ky.: Westminster/John Knox Press.

Rosenbaum, Max. 1983. *Compliant Behavior: Beyond Obedience to Authority*. New York: Human Sciences Press.

Stivers, Robert L., Christine E. Gudorf, Alice Frazer Evans, and Robert A. Evans. 1989. *Christian Ethics*. New York: Orbis Books.

Stone, Howard W. 1989. "The Pastoral Care of John Keble, Oxford Reformer." *The Journal of Pastoral Care* 43, no. 1 (spring): 2–15.

Sykes, Gresham, and Sheldon L. Messinger. 1960. "The Inmate Social System." In *Theoretical Studies in Social Organization of the Prison*, edited by the Social Science Research Center, 5–19. United States of America: Social Science Research Center.

Telleen, Sharon. 1980. "The Church as a Support to Families Under Stress." In *Health and Healing: Ministry of the Church*, edited by Henry L. Lettermann, 91–107. Madison, Wis.: Wheat Ridge Foundation.

Unger, Merrill. 1957. *Unger's Bible Dictionary*. Chicago: Moody Press.

Williams, Janet B. W., ed. 1987. *Diagnostic Criteria from DSM-III-R*. Washington, D.C.: American Psychiatric Association.

Wilson, Marlene. 1976. *The Effective Management of Volunteer Programs*. Boulder, Colo.: Volunteer Management Associates.

Index

Purves, Andrew
  on Christ's lordship over suffering,
    73, 74
  on compassion, 86

Rahe, R. H., 13, 15
Rasmussen, Larry, 92
Rockview. *See* State Correctional
    Institution at Rockview
Rosenbaum, Max, 35

Scriptures
  examining change using, 9
  Hebrew, 67, 68, 69
  importance of instruction in, 84
Self-actualization, 19
Seventh-day Adventist Church, 98
Sin, Genesis account of, *xii*
Social Readjustment Scale, 14–15
  and imprisonment, 15
Social support, 30
Society
  called by Christ to aid oppressed, *xii*
  concern over prisons, *xi*
  images of successful prison ministry,
    6
  and inmate education, 57
  reentering, 55, 61–62.
  for touching others' lives, *xii*
  understanding, 67
Spiritual growth. *See* Inmate personal
    growth; Spirituality
Spirituality
  inmate, 41
  models for inmate, *vii*
  of prison chaplains, 6
  and stress, 13
State Correctional Institution at Camp
    Hill, 40, 55
State Correctional Institution at
    Rockview, *ix*

chaplain's ministry to condemned
    inmate, 121–26
contract clergy in, 3
disturbances in, 40
as execution site, 1, 60
mood of, prior to executions, 60
population of, 3, 37
reaction to Camp Hill riot, 55
volunteers in, 3
Stress. *See also* Inmate stressors
  and burnout, 16
  diagnostic reporting of
    Diagnostic and Statistical Manual
      of Mental Disorders, 15, 16
    Global Assessment of
      Functioning Scale, 16
    Psychosocial Stressor Scale, 15
  enduring stressors, 15
  magnified by incarceration, 15, 20
  predominantly acute stressors, 15
  research data on, 13–15
  and self-esteem, 22–23
  and spiritual growth, 13
Sykes, Gresham, 24

Telleen, Sharon, 22–23
Teresa, Mother, 90
Thomas à Kempis, 76

Unger, Merrill, 68

Westberg, Jill, 95

Zettlemoyer, Keith
  author's conversation with, 121–26
  execution of, 121
  remorse of, 122
  spirituality of, 122–25